Cartes depicting a man and a woman occupy this small leather travelling carte-de-visite case produced by Edwards & Jones of London. The case dates from c.1870.

Victorian Cartes-de-Visite

Robin and Carol Wichard

Shire Publications

Cover: *(Centre) A carefully tinted introductory album carte produced by W. B. Prince, Photographic Publisher, of London, dating from the mid 1860s. (Top left) The 'Children of the Battlefield' carte (see page 61). (Top right) A fine portrait of a girl (probably in her teens) taken c.1864 by H. P. Robinson. (Bottom left) An attractive hand-tinted portrait of Princess Alice taken by John Mayall of London on 1st June 1861. (Bottom right) 'Mr Coverdale's carriage and driver' (see page 80).*

ACKNOWLEDGEMENTS
A book like this inevitably draws heavily on the work of other writers, and it is hoped that the acknowledgements given in the text, and the fuller references made to their work in the further reading section, will be accepted as a token of the authors' gratitude for the inspiration provided. In the United States, Henry Deeks proved extremely supportive and was even prepared to send a box of cartes across the Atlantic 'on trust'. In England, a tremendous debt of gratitude is owed to Anne Scott, who has sought out many of the images in this book and then sold them to us at a price which can have allowed her little profit. Both Henry Deeks and Anne Scott represent the very best of dealers, with a real passion for their chosen subject. The excellent photographs throughout this book (and on the front cover) have been taken by Norman Stanley of Minehead, Somerset, and are evidence of his skill and patience. Finally, thanks are due to Richard O'Sullivan for his thorough and perceptive proofreading.

Published in 1999 by Shire Publications Ltd, Cromwell House, Church Street, Princes Risborough, Buckinghamshire HP27 9AA, UK. Website: www.shirebooks.co.uk
Copyright © 1999 by Robin and Carol Wichard. First published 1999. Number 13 in the History in Camera series. ISBN 0 7478 0433 8.
Robin and Carol Wichard are hereby identified as the authors of this work in accordance with Section 77 of the Copyright, Designs and Patents Act, 1988.

British Library Cataloguing in Publication Data: Wichard, Robin. Victorian cartes-de-visite. – (History in camera; 13) 1. Carte de visite photographs – History. 2. Carte de visite photographs – Collectors and collecting. I. Title. II. Wichard, Carol. 770.9'034. ISBN 0 7478 0433 8.

Printed in Great Britain by CIT Printing Services Ltd, Press Buildings, Merlins Bridge, Haverfordwest, Pembrokeshire SA61 1XF.

Contents

Introduction 5

The history of photography 6

The carte-de-visite and portrait photography 21

Celebrity cartes 33

Photographing the cycle of life 44

Special occasions, events and places 57

Cartes-de-visite and art 69

The carte-de-visite in the home 74

Collecting, dating and preserving cartes-de-visite 85

Further reading 99

Places to visit 100

Index 101

Ghémar Frères, Photographes du Roi Bruxelles

Ghémar Frères of Brussels took this beautiful portrait of Princess Louise c.1861.
The photograph was published in Britain by the firm of A. Marion & Company of
London. When sold originally, this image was protected by a thin sheet of plain
tissue paper that could be folded back in order to view it properly.

Introduction

Agatha Christie's popular hero Hercule Poirot once posed the question 'Why do people keep photographs?' His conclusion was that there are three reasons – vanity, sentiment and to help solve a murder. There is now a fourth reason – for the pleasure of collecting. Few types of photograph offer more scope for the collector than the carte-de-visite.

The introduction of the carte-de-visite in 1854 brought affordable portrait photography into the homes of ordinary people for the first time. The mysteries of the world beyond were now systematically photographed and made available in a way never previously possible. The public seized on the carte-de-visite with an enthusiasm never seen before, or since! At the height of the carte-de-visite's popularity (referred to as 'cartomania'), between three and four hundred million cartes a year were being sold, leaving us with a huge legacy.

The number, and diversity, of surviving images mean that the carte-de-visite has often been overlooked. There is, in consequence, tremendous scope for collectors, regardless of the amount of money they have to spend. Almost no aspect of Victorian life was left unrecorded, giving a unique insight into Victorian society. The importance of the carte-de-visite is now becoming recognised, as the growth of major photographic collections attests.

This book is intended to introduce the reader to carte-de-visite photographs, the context in which they were produced, and the pleasures of collecting them.

A sixth-plate daguerreo-type of a young child from the late 1850s produced at the studio of Marcus Root in Philadelphia. The plate size refers to the propor-tion of a full-size photo-graphic plate used for the image – in this case one-sixth of a whole plate. The best plates were manufac-tured in France and obtaining a good one was important since poorer quality plates dramatically affected the appearance of the final product.

The history of photography

The origins of photography lie in an instrument called the *camera obscura,* which was commonly used to project an image on to paper. The resulting image could then be traced and used by artists to provide the basic structure for landscapes and their scenes. The breakthrough needed to create a viable photograph was some method of holding, or 'fixing', the image.

In 1827, the Frenchman Joseph Nicéphore Niépce used a *camera obscura* and a pewter plate to produce the world's first photograph – the view from a window of his house in Gras. In 1829 Niépce went into partnership with a Parisian artist, Louis-Jacques-Mandé Daguerre. Although Niépce died in 1833, Daguerre went on to perfect the world's first practical photographic process, producing an image, on a polished metal plate, known as a daguerreotype. Daguerre was awarded an annual pension from the French government in return for the rights to his process, which the government wished to present to the world (except Britain!) as a gift. In August 1839, a manual was produced, giving instructions for the daguerreotype process, which was widely circulated. As early as 1841, the studio of N. P. Lerebours began production of the first photographic 'art studies' (nudes).

The daguerreotype image was extremely fragile and easily damaged. To preserve it, the daguerreotype was supplied covered with a sheet of clear glass which was raised above the image by the insertion of a decorative brass mat between the cover and the image itself. The whole package was then sealed with tape and placed inside a specially made, leather-covered, wood-framed box, or in an embossed plastic case (known as a 'Union' case).

A method of reducing the exposure times enough to make portrait photography possible was introduced by another Frenchman, Antoine Claudet (who lived and worked in Britain). There was tremendous interest in this new artistic medium and at the French Product Exposition in 1844 the work of almost one thousand daguerreotype artists was exhibited. Within weeks of the publication of Daguerre's manual, Prussian optician Theodore Dorffel was building and selling daguerreotype equipment. This led to a number of key developments in the process, most notably a portrait lens developed by Josef Petzal and manufactured by the firm of Voightlander. Daguerreotype equipment produced

A beautiful quarter-plate daguerreotype of an unidentified (probably American) couple dating from the late 1840s. The image is still housed within its original protective case made of leather-covered wood. Both the unusual 'scallop' mat, which was produced from the late 1840s until c.1851, and the narrow brass preserver, which holds the various components of the daguerreotype together, help to date this image.

A good example of a superbly moulded thermoplastic photographic case, known as a Union case, for a quarter-plate image dating from the late 1850s. This design was entitled 'Money Musk' or 'The Country Dance' and was produced by Littlefield Parsons & Company.

by Alphonse Giroux of France had reached Italy by November 1839.

The only country not to benefit from Daguerre's free gift to the world was Britain, where Daguerre took out a patent on the process. Few British photographers were willing to pay the licence fee and in consequence the process was restricted to relatively few professional portrait artists, such as Richard Beard and Antoine Claudet. Although Beard's studio was the first to produce hand-coloured daguerreotypes, and it was Beard and his associate John Goddard who developed the first effective accelerator, which dramatically reduced exposure times, it was Antoine Claudet who emerged as the more successful – especially after 1849 when Beard was declared bankrupt. Claudet was soon producing images for the *Illustrated London News* and was courted by the rich and famous in both France and Britain.

Regent Street became the centre of daguerreotype photography in London, with a number of studios operating, including those of Beard and an American, John Mayall, who was to become a central figure in British photography throughout the second half of the nineteenth century.

Details of Daguerre's process reached the United States in September 1839 on board Brunel's steamship *Great Western*. The process was enthusiastically embraced and, by 1841, there were hundreds of Americans engaged in daguerreotype photography. The Frenchman François Gouraud acted as Daguerre's agent in the United States and, through lectures and demonstrations, played a major role in encouraging the rapid expansion of the process. In 1841, the studio of John Plumbe opened and within four years the business had expanded to include a chain of fourteen studios. Plumbe also began to assemble a collection of 'famous portraits' – an idea taken up later by Mathew Brady (probably the best-known American photographer of the period). Brady opened his first studio in 1844 opposite the P. T. Barnum museum. Like Plumbe, he set out to make a photographic record of the famous people of the day, which he termed his 'Gallery of Illustrious Americans', a collection later extensively copied and issued commercially as cartes-de-visite in the early 1860s. By 1850, there were almost one hundred daguerreotype studios in New York alone.

Meanwhile, back in England, William Henry Fox Talbot had resolved to try to 'fix' permanently the images seen in his artist's *camera obscura*. As early as 1833, Fox Talbot had noted, from the work of chemists, that silver nitrate was sensitive to light. He began to experiment and, by reducing the amount of salt present, was able to make paper treated with the chemical far more sensitive. Since salt was seen to reduce sensitivity, Fox Talbot used a strong solution to 'fix' his images, or 'photographic drawings' as he called them. In February 1835 Fox Talbot discovered the principle of the paper negative, recording in his notebook that 'if the paper is transparent, the first drawing may serve as an object, to produce a second drawing in which the lights and shadows would be reversed'.

Further experimentation with chemical washes during the bright summer of 1835 enabled Fox Talbot to reduce exposure times to around ten minutes. Owing to other commitments, Fox Talbot did little to develop his discoveries further until, in January 1839, he heard of Daguerre's process. Fox Talbot immediately arranged an exhibition of his 'photographic drawings' at the Royal Institute in London (25th January 1839) and presented papers at the Royal Society on 31st January and again on 20th February in which he published a description of his photographic process. By 1840, a newly inspired Fox Talbot had discovered that only a brief exposure to light was required to produce a latent image on sensitised paper which could be revealed by the addition of a solution of silver nitrate / gallic acid. This produced a negative, which was then waxed to make it translucent, from which positive prints could be made. Fox Talbot named his process 'calotype' (from a Greek word meaning 'beautiful') but they are commonly known as 'Talbotypes' in his honour.

In 1841, Fox Talbot patented the process and licences were required by all except amateurs. The patent rights were relinquished by Fox Talbot in 1852 but by then the process (like that of Daguerre) was about to be superseded.

The paper Fox Talbot used for printing was relatively coarse and the fibres tended to limit fine detail. A better medium would be something smooth like glass if a suitable, sensitised material could be made to adhere to it. In 1847,

A first-class ambrotype in almost mint condition by an unknown photographer, showing an unidentified young woman. The oval mat was one of the most popular mat types during the second half of the 1850s. The ornately decorated brass preserver with its reinforced corners dates from the late 1850s onwards and, together with the mat, suggests that this image also dates from the late 1850s.

Abel Niépce de Saint-Victor (a cousin of Nicéphore Niépce) found that egg-white – albumen – provided that suitable base. However, in 1851, English sculptor Frederick Scott Archer devised a new method using collodion (a mixture of gun-cotton dissolved in ether). As the solution was poured over a glass plate, the ether began to evaporate, leaving a tacky residue that could be sensitised, then exposed, while still wet (hence the process became known as 'wet-plate' photography). If the plate was allowed to dry, it lost almost all of its sensitivity. Exposure required only seconds, making the process ideal for portraiture and more general photography. Scott Archer freely published details of his process and, in consequence, gained no income from his work. He died in poverty in 1857.

In 1852, Scott Archer had published details of a further development which involved whitening the negative and providing a black background that caused the negative image to appear as a positive. This was known as the 'collodion positive' or, more commonly, the 'ambrotype', a name given by the American photographer Marcus Root, who based it on the Greek word *ambrotos* meaning 'immortal'. In the United States, this process had also been noted, and patented, by James Cutting of Boston, Massachusetts.

This sixth-plate tintype image of an American soldier is by an unknown photographer. Both the ornate preserver and the heavily embossed mat date the photograph to the 1860s. A small amount of rouge has been used to accentuate the colour on the face.

In Europe at least, the ambrotype process, requiring no licence and little skill, soon eclipsed the popularity of the daguerreotype and, in no time at all, framed ambrotypes were being offered for as little as sixpence, which truly made photography available to all levels of society – even the poor. Ambrotype images, like daguerreotypes, needed the protection of a glass cover and decorative brass mats. There was now a demand, however, for cheaper cases commensurate with the price of the finished image. This price reduction was achieved through a reduction in quality. The most expensive cases remained the plastic 'Union' cases first patented by the American Samuel Peck on 3rd October 1854, but cheaper, wooden-framed cases were soon being manufactured, covered in embossed cardboard, papier-mâché or, more rarely, leather.

In 1853, the French photographer Adolphé Martin described a variation of the collodion positive process which substituted a sheet of black, enamelled tinplate for the sheet of glass. Sold as a 'ferrotype' (or 'tintype' in the United States), this format became very popular in the 1860s. During the 1860 presidential campaign, some 300,000 small campaign badges were produced,

A beautiful portrait by Disdéri & Company of Paris. Disdéri patented the carte-de-visite format in 1854. This portrait, taken in the early 1860s, has been carefully composed so that the draped material echoes the line of the subject's dress, thereby diagonally dissecting the image.

each containing a small tintype image of one of the candidates, Abraham Lincoln. The American Civil War, which followed Lincoln's victory, provided a huge market for tintypes, and photographers flocked to the rapidly expanding military camps. The process was widely used by itinerant photographers and by stallholders at beaches and fairgrounds, where it remained in use well into the twentieth century. Although tintypes lacked the quality of ambrotypes and daguerreotypes, they were cheap and easy to produce. The tintype never achieved the same level of popularity in Europe that it achieved in America and, in consequence, the process was often referred to as 'the American process'.

The drawback of all these processes remained the fact that they produced one-off products. Although Fox Talbot's negatives, and the glass negatives, could be printed on to paper, the loss of detail rendered the final product relatively unattractive. In 1850, Louis-Désiré Blanquart-Evrard described his research which showed that if the paper was coated in albumen with ammonium chloride before being sensitised it produced a fine, smooth surface capable of reproducing the finest details. This process was straightforward but time-consuming and therefore made paper prints more expensive until a method was devised that allowed a number of pictures to be taken on a single plate, thereby greatly reducing the cost. These small prints could then each be glued on to a piece of card 2.5 by 4 inches (63 by 100 mm) – slightly larger than the print itself. The final product was of similar size to the popular visiting cards used at the time. This led to the prints becoming known as 'cartes-de-visite'.

The first patent for the carte-de-visite format was taken out by Disdéri of Paris on 27th November 1854 and few would contest that the worldwide adoption and popularity of the format were due to his initiative. However, Disdéri did not invent the format. Indeed, no-one is sure who can claim that honour although there are a number of contenders. The French journal *La Lumière* of October 1854 claimed that

> E. Delensert and Count Aguado had an original idea for the use of small portraits. Up to now, visiting cards carried only the name, address, and sometimes the title of the persons whom they represented. Why should not the name be replaced by a portrait?

However, a letter dated 24th August 1851 in the same journal, from a Marseilles photographer named Louis Dodero, suggested that photographs could be used on visiting cards, passports, hunting licences and many other official documents.

As Helmut Gernsheim notes, however, *The Practical Mechanic's Journal* of 1855 suggested that the format had originated in the United States.

> The Yankee man of fashion, it is said, does not descend to the prosaic plan of engraving his name on his visiting card, but fills his card-case with photographs of himself, which he hands [out] instead.

After the introduction of the carte-de-visite in the late 1850s, some case manufacturers continued to produce cases for the new format. This example shows the plush velvet lining of the case, and the mat and preserver – although these were not strictly necessary. The case dates from the early 1860s. The manufacturer is unknown.

When collected from the photographer's studio, cartes were often presented in protective card sleeves. This ornately embossed example comes from the studio of Alexander Bassano, Regent Street, London. The photographs shown were in the sleeve when purchased and help to date it to the mid 1870s.

Although cartes-de-visite were cheap, attempts were made to maintain the impression of luxury and expense. Although the format did not require a protective frame, a small number of manufacturers continued to produce both wooden-framed and plastic cases for the carte-de-visite although these are now quite uncommon. The costs of cartes-de-visite are very well documented since many photographers printed details of their prices on the back of their mounts. The firm of H. Wilcox advertised cartes 'from 5/- to 1 Guinea pr. Dozen according to the quality'. In the United States, the firm of Egbert G. Fowx of Baltimore, Maryland, advertised cartes at '$2.00 per dozen or $4.00 if coloured'.

The American Civil War created a demand for cheap portraits either to carry as a reminder of friends and family at home or to send home as reassurance after a prolonged period at the front. Cartes-de-visite fitted the bill perfectly and tintypists sought ways of converting their images to the carte-de-visite format. In the United States, tintypes were placed in specially produced paper frames in the standard carte size, embossed with a variety of emblems, often patriotic. Such frames were also commonly embossed with the words 'Potter's Patent March 7 1865'. Small tintype images, known as 'gems', were introduced

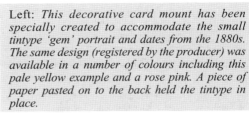

Left: *This decorative card mount has been specially created to accommodate the small tintype 'gem' portrait and dates from the 1880s. The same design (registered by the producer) was available in a number of colours including this pale yellow example and a rose pink. A piece of paper pasted on to the back held the tintype in place.*

Above: *George W. Godfrey & Company of Main Street, Rochester, New York, cleverly adapted this 'gem' portrait (taken using Wing's Patent Multiplying Camera) to the carte-de-visite format. The portrait is held in a small brass preserver by two lugs which are stuck through the card mount and bent over to hold the image in place.*

Left: *A tintype portrait c.1864 by an unidentified American photographer in an embossed patriotic mount. The American eagle astride the portrait clearly indicates the photographer's allegiance to the Union during the American Civil War. Below the portrait, military standards, artillery pieces and a drum can be seen.*

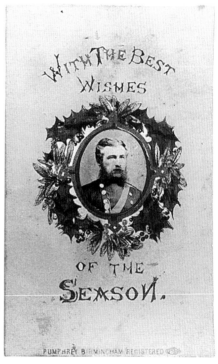

Left: *The backplate of an American tintype by the company of Spencer & Downs. The card is backed with a piece of paper that held the tinplate in place. The backing paper (printed by 'Chronicle Print') also detailed the various prices charged.*

Right: *An unusual image using a mount registered by Pumphrey of Birmingham. The centre has been punched in order to raise the image. Note that the 'N' of 'season' has been reversed. The photographer is unknown.*

by Simon Wing in 1860. Wing patented a multilens camera which allowed a large number of gems to be produced on a single plate. These were adapted to the carte-de-visite format by inserting them into mounting cards with oval windows cut out to accommodate them.

As the popularity of the carte format increased, novelty cartes were introduced. Specially printed mounts offered birthday or Christmas greetings. Others had the appropriate sentiment incorporated into the image itself, although at least one example, by Dodson of Swindon, had the greeting printed in reverse because of the effects of printing from a negative. The production of festive cartes became a profitable business and many photographers offered the service. The art photographers Harrison's of Falmouth offered a whole range of services including 'your own photograph made into a Christmas carte or Cabinet – a very effective novelty'.

Above left: *In this portrait (taken c.1861 by an unknown photographer) a seasonal senti-ment has been printed on the bottom of the mount. Although unusual, many studios offered this service. Other appropriate sentiments (such as birthday greetings) were also available.*

Above right: *Many studios supplied their photographs with a protective layer of tissue paper glued to the back of the card and folded across the front of the photograph. In this example – by H. Montague Cooper of Taunton, Somerset – the covering tissue has the photographer's details printed on it.*

An advertising carte prepared by the studio of Harrison's of Falmouth, Cornwall. The company provided an extensive range of services (including using the permanent carbon – or chromotype – process). This carte-de-visite advertises the company's services as art photographers.

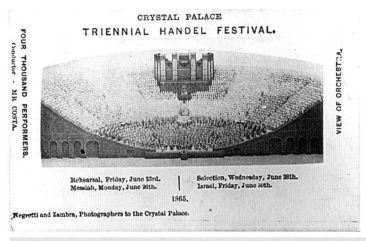

A colossal organ dominates this photograph of the orchestra of four thousand musicians depicted on this unusual carte by Negretti & Zambra on the occasion of the Triennial Handel Festival at the Crystal Palace, London, in 1865.

Cartes could also be used to advertise products. Harrison's of Falmouth produced a number of attractive cartes advertising their company. In 1876, the London shop of Peter Robinson put together a series of cartes depicting their gowns worn by models. Details of the prices and materials were printed on the reverse side of the mount.

There seemed to be no limit to the uses to which the carte-de-visite could be

put. On the occasion of the Triennial Handel Festival in 1865 at the Crystal Palace, a carte was produced by Negretti & Zambra showing the entire orchestra of four thousand musicians. The carte also bore the details of all rehearsals and performances as an aide-mémoire to those involved.

Other novelty gimmicks (often of limited appeal and duration) included the Diamond Cameo Portrait introduced by F. R. Window in October 1864. Instead of a single image, the Diamond Cameo had four small portraits, each showing a different view of the sitter's head. The arrangement of these small portraits in a diamond pattern gave the

A carte by Adolphe Beau of Regent Street, London, taken using the Diamond Cameo Portrait format introduced in October 1864. Each small portrait was punched into relief and the carte is also embossed with the photographer's mark.

ADOLPHE BEAU, 283, REGENT ST. LONDON W

A 'permanent photograph' using the chromotype process and taken by E. Goodfellow of Wincanton, Somerset. Costing half as much again as an ordinary carte-de-visite, and with a tendency to curl, the process never gained extensive popularity.

format its name. The oval containing each image was punched into relief to emphasise the portrait. Although some 400,000 licences for this format were reputed to have been issued, it never attracted widespread interest. The photographer H. Wilcox offered Diamond Cameo Portraits 'from 12/- to 18/- per Dozen', which could help explain its unpopularity. Even less popular was the Bi-medallion, introduced in 1870, which offered two portraits side by side.

Photographers were also continually working to overcome the problems of image fading. One of the most commonly used methods was the carbon print process, introduced by J. W. Swan in 1864, and popular in Britain and western Europe in the late 1870s. This is also referred to as the permanent carbon process. Cartes produced

These two images show how a photographer was able to 'restore' damaged images by careful editing. The first image simply shows the extent of the damage as the surface of an ambrotype has begun to peel away, taking the image with it. Since the damage cannot be reversed, it is necessary for the photographer to use vignetting to remove the worst effects of the damage. Only a small area in the bottom left-hand corner remains as evidence of the original damage. The photographer is unknown.

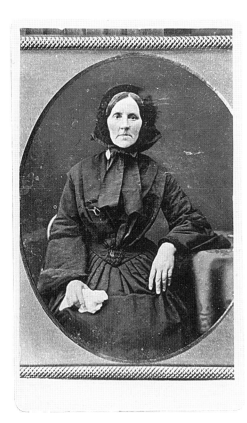

A carte from an unidentified photographer copying a daguerreotype of the late 1850s. The brass oval mat frames the portrait and shows that the photographer used lighting from the left-hand side rather than direct light (which would have shown the image as a negative). The plain brass preserver (which held the image, mat and glass together) can be seen at the top and bottom of the photograph.

by this process were priced up to fifty per cent higher than ordinary cartes, which possibly restricted their appeal, as did their tendency to curl.

In addition to experimenting with new formats, many photographers offered reprints from negatives held in stock and many also offered to copy daguerreotypes and ambrotypes as well. Sometimes this service afforded the opportunity to repair damage by means of careful retouching or vignetting. The American photographer H. S. Deibert of Schuylkill Haven, Pennsylvania, also offered:

> Frames, Cases and Photograph Albums at prices lower than can be bought elsewhere. Also Photographs framed to order. Rosewood and Gilt Mouldings for framing pictures. Also Galvanising done to order, such as Watches, Watch Chains &c.

Egbert G. Fowx of Baltimore, Maryland, even promised:

> Amateurs taught this beautiful art in all its various branches.

The carte-de-visite and portrait photography

The introduction of the carte-de-visite meant that photographic portraits were now within the grasp of almost everyone in society, regardless of their social status. However, far from heralding a new beginning in portraiture, the new format clung rigidly to tradition – despite the fears of artists such as Paul Delaroche, who, when catching his first sight of a photograph, is reputed to have announced, 'From today painting is dead!'

When the first commercial photographic studio opened in Britain on 23rd March 1841 (at 301 Regent Street, London) the traditions of portraiture were already long established. Photography was keen to be seen as a form of art and therefore embraced these traditions but, in doing so, became bound by artistic convention. It is no coincidence that the backplates of many carte-de-visite photographs vignette the photographer's name and address within an outline of an artist's palette and brushes to emphasise the link. Some such photographers even emphasise their roles as miniature painters as well by making explicit reference to that function in their credits.

As in portrait painting, the portrait photographer's primary function was to portray the sitter in the best light possible, highlighting the best features and concealing less flattering blemishes. The portrait was also expected to reveal something of the 'whole person'. *The Photographic News* of 3rd November 1876 observed that the aim of portraiture was 'to secure a portrait of a man in his completeness, mind and body, instead of a mere mask of his physical present-ment'.

While the true character of the sitter needed to be represented, it was equally important that the process was seen to be flattering. Photographers soon came up with a range of techniques to facilitate this aim, as shown in this cartoon from 'Punch' (18th January 1862). The caption accompanying this cartoon reads: 'Dodge of Little Sperks, showing how Parties below the Middle Height, by the use of Miniature Background Furniture, may gain a more Imposing Stature in the Carte de Visite'.

The detail and expression captured in this superb, vignetted portrait by John Mayall of London clearly show how deserved his reputation was. Technical difficulties limit the size of the head in this portrait.

Mayall,Photo   London&Brighton

The need to reveal the true character of the sitter was seen by Cornelius Jabez Hughes (in his book *The Principles and Practice of Photography*, 1859) as a priority.

> The primary object should be to produce a characteristic likeness, and the second one to render it as pleasing as possible by judicious selection of the view of the face and the pose of the figure, so as, without sacrificing character, to bring out the good points and conceal the less favourable ones.

In reality, however, 'character' tended to follow the long-established stereotypes of modesty and purity for women and dignity and strength for men – hence the similarity between so many early photographic portraits. A broad smile might be interpreted as a sign of frivolity and, therefore, serious, calm and dignified facial expressions became the norm.

After expression, pose was the next major indicator of character. The pose chosen had to be appropriate to the sitter's age, stature and manner and was to be as graceful as could be achieved. Great efforts were taken by photographers to choose poses which would reduce the impact of any physical deficiencies

Seated at an elaborate desk laden with books, this sitter is shown in a typical three-quarter-face pose. The open book clearly indicates literacy and education (valued qualities). The careful placing of the hand on the crucifix suspended from a beaded necklace, giving prominence to the wedding ring, is also deliberate although the exact significance can only be guessed at. The portrait is by J. Hawke of Devon.

A. L. Henderson of London Bridge took this portrait of a fashionably dressed gentleman. The edge of a painted backdrop can be clearly seen on the left, and the base of a neck clamp is visible behind the subject. The pose shows how much latitude was extended to men, as compared to women, with the umbrella and hat used as props.

(for example lack of height). Such characteristics as height and girth could be altered visually by the choice of clothing worn. H. J. Rogers, writing in 1872, noted that 'long longitudinal stripes in a lady's dress cause her to appear taller...one row of flounces makes her appear shorter in stature, and continues to decrease in apparent height as the flounces, or ruffles, are added upwards on the dress'. In the end, such embellishments attracted the attention of the satirical

The great difficulty in Photography is to get the Sitter to assume a Pleasing Expression of Countenance—Jones, however, thinks that, in this instance, he has been extremely successful.

For the customer, the final product was all important, but the lengths to which some photographers went in order to gain an appropriate 'pleasing expression of countenance' was satirised by 'Punch', as in this cartoon published on 7th June 1862.

magazine *Punch*.

Men were afforded rather more latitude than women in their choice of pose (legs could be crossed or elbows thrust out by placing the hands on the hips). Such individuality of posture served to emphasise the importance and power of the sitter.

The pose of women was required to reflect their natural poise and grace.

This splendid full-length portrait of Mrs Duffield by Australian photographer J. Duryea of Adelaide shows how the skilful use of vignetting serves to focus the eye on the central figure. Note the long watch-chain worn around her brooch rather than her neck.

A small boy with a drum and his pet dog must have posed numerous potential problems for the studio of Chancellor of Sackville Street, Dublin, but the result is clearly worthwhile. By standing the child on a chair, the photographer has avoided having to work the camera at low level. The carte is inscribed on the reverse 'For my dear Aunt Kate from her Godson'.

Arms were to be kept close to the body, maintaining gentle curves, in contrast to the aggressive and angular poses of the men. The majority of poses adopted by women involved a three-quarter view with the eyes following the direction of the head – a pose thought to emphasise the gentler qualities of expression. Often it was difficult for the photographer to achieve the desired pose without some contact with the sitter, although man-handling of sitters was regarded as a sign of a low-class establishment. It was also difficult on occasion to overcome the wishes of the sitters (and their entourage). John (J. E.) Mayall asserted his authority with a tactful sign hung in his studio which announced that 'Sitters are requested to place themselves as much as possible in the hands of the artist'.

To ensure that the chosen pose was maintained, a variety of devices was employed to hold the sitter in place. Support could be achieved by leaning the sitter on, or against, a prop such as a balustrade or pillar. Posing stands were regularly used to support both standing and seated poses. The wide crinoline dresses of the early to mid 1860s effectively covered the bases of these stands. Where this was not possible, the bottom of a full-length curtain could be discreetly drawn across to cover it. Despite such measures, many photographs of both men and children show the base of a posing stand on the floor behind the sitter's feet.

The impression of character could be further enhanced by the use of studio props and backdrops. Such measures also directed attention away from aspects of the face, figure or clothing that were unflattering. Although some photographers continued to favour plain backdrops, elaborately painted scenes, echoing the tastes of the 'Old Masters', were widely favoured. Some

photographers working in areas with strong naval or military traditions employed suitably inspiring backdrops. Most photographers, however, used impressions of wealthy drawing rooms (with suitable furnishings to complete the illusion and windows looking out on to parklands or formal gardens) or rural settings (accentuated by the judicious placing of rustic benches or gates). Both types served to maintain the traditions established in formal portraiture many

A portrait of an unidentified woman and child. The woman rests a hand on the chair to help hold her pose and the child stands on the chair in order to give her height. In comparison with the preceding portraits, this image is dominated by the complex, and rather crowded, painted backdrop.

generations earlier.

Such associations with formal portraiture were deliberately fostered. They served to demonstrate the artistic credentials of the photographer. For the customer, such backgrounds allowed them the pretence of moving beyond their normal social constraints, appearing instead with the trappings of wealth, education and status often completely at odds with the reality of their position. The whole impression was further exaggerated by the expectation that sitters would dress appropriately for their portraits (that is, in their Sunday best). Cleverly placed props could then be used to draw attention to certain attributes – for example a book placed under the hand of the sitter implied literacy, highly valued in the days before compulsory education.

That such a charade should conflict so obviously with the desire to create a true likeness of the character of the sitter does not appear to have created any substantial problems although a few photographers did express their concerns. Oscar Rejlander regarded painted backdrops 'as an illegitimate mingling of the unrealities of conventional art with the truth of photography which must ever result in incongruity'. However, such incongruities persisted and only rarely did people choose to be photographed in their normal, working attire. At the peak of the carte-de-visite's popularity, commercial cartes of local fisher girls

were produced in coastal areas for sale to tourists as souvenirs. Some people such as policemen, firemen and railway employees, proud of the social status implied by their working clothes, chose to be photographed in their uniforms. However, such cases remained the exception rather than the rule and cartes of people in their working clothes are therefore unusual today.

The carte-de-visite format made it possible for many more

The work of itinerant photographers made an important and substantial contribution to the body of surviving portraiture. Despite the poorly painted (and excessively wrinkled) backdrop secured at the base by a plank, the sitter is proud and confident.

Itinerant street musicians were rarely photographed, which make this pair, with their well-worn clothes, an unusual commission for photographer Henry Stiles of West Kensington, London. The fact that the musicians were photographed in the street and not in the studio suggests that the image may not have been intended for the musicians themselves.

In this portrait by R. Cade of Ipswich, Suffolk, the simplicity of the backdrop and the carpet draws the eye towards the subject at centre. The hand resting on the chair helped the person to balance. By grasping the watch-chain, the arm could also be held steady, thereby avoiding any movements that could cause blurring of the image.

people to have a full-length portrait taken of themselves than was possible before. Traditionally, in painting, full-length portraits were restricted to the wealthiest patrons and, as late as the mid nineteenth century, still carried connotations of class and social stature. This new-found freedom was not without its price, however. The American photographer M. A. Root, writing in 1864, noted: 'The carte-de-visite...makes larger requisitions on the operator's knowledge of art...than any other phase of photography.' One difficulty remained the fact that the camera distorted colour representation – green, yellow, orange and red all appeared dark while pale blue appeared white, rendering the contrasts in photographs of the period rather more striking than surviving garments suggest. These problems were not fully overcome until the late 1890s. The photographer therefore needed to guide his sitters away from choices of clothing likely to create major problems. As early as 1846, Dr Andrew Wynter encouraged daguerreotype sitters to avoid white as much as possible.

> Many a good picture is spoiled by the spottiness occasioned by the powerful action of this colour upon the plate. Violets have the same effect upon it. A lady takes her sitting in a purple dress and is astonished to find herself in white muslin in her portrait ... The very best kind of dress to wear is of any material upon which there is a play of light or shade. Plaids always look well.

In the 1850s John Mayall handed prospective sitters a card entitled 'Suggestions for Dress'. He informed ladies that:

> Dark silks and satins are best for dress; shot silk, checked, striped or figured material provided that they not be too light, and colours to be avoided are white, pale blue and pink. The only dark colour to be avoided is black velvet.

Clearly the difficulties presented by large expanses of white rendered white weddings a photographer's nightmare; fortunately white was not widely worn by brides until later in the century. Even so, such photographs would require considerable skill and no small amount of retouching.

A relatively small number of vignetted head shots were also produced in the early 1860s but deficiencies in the lens made it difficult to reproduce heads that filled the whole print area. Such early head shots were more popular in the United States than in Britain. As lens quality improved, however, so the head size increased so that by the mid 1870s the head could nearly fill the print area. Another technical difficulty with head shots concerned lighting. Reproducing the detail of a sitter's face required strong lighting but this also served to highlight blemishes. These could be reduced by retouching either the image or the negative. Retouching the negative became the preferred method after 1870 but was relatively uncommon before then. Another method, known as Mezzo Tinto (patented by Carl Meinerth in Newburyport, Massachusetts, in 1867), involved placing a plate glass or thin sheet of mica between the negative and the printing paper. This served to soften the image.

One shortcoming of carte-de-visite portraits remained their lack of colour. Although some photographers refused to colour their images, many did respond to the perceived need. Water-based paints were used which penetrated the surface of the image, giving relative permanence without obscuring the detail beneath. In many cases, impressive results were obtained by the skilled use of

Mr Nelson of Bayswater, London, took this portrait of actor John Parry in female attire. The over-large polkadot pattern that covers the entire outfit suggests a parody of an unfashionable woman. To be fashionable, the hat should be worn lower at the front, and it is of a style not usually tied with ribbons. The trimming would be rather more restrained than is evident in John Parry's parody.

A comic portrait of three friends by German photographer Jacob Kaunitzer dating from the early 1870s. Note the careful positioning of the cigars. A variation on this theme by Brookes of Manchester shows three male figures looking over a studio 'bridge'. The reverse side of the carte has another photograph showing the same three characters from the rear.

J. KAUNITZER.

" *Public Nuisance,*" *January 1st 1866.*

Both the identity of the photographer and the location of this curious image are unfortunately lost. Groups of musicians are unusual subjects for portraiture but the placement of empty(?) bottles and the mixture of clothing suggests that this may be a satirical carte, possibly poking gentle fun at some of the small town bands which could, on occasion, boast more enthusiasm than talent.

The company of Hills & Saunders clearly targeted their clientele by establishing branches at Harrow, Eton, Oxford, Cambridge and London. This photograph, taken at their Harrow branch, shows a Harrow School football team in the late 1870s. Harrow football is played by teams of ten men and is rather more physical than its popular counterpart.

A pirated copy of a carte depicting the
first England cricket team to tour Australia in the early 1860s. The full team
is shown along with Mr Mallam, the
Australian representative. The backdrop depicts a pavilion and the edge of
the sheet can be seen over the shoulder
of Mr Bennett, the player standing on
the extreme left. The bats and balls
have been positioned to illustrate the
strengths of the individual players.

a very small range of colours. These
achievements were even more
impressive considering that many of the
larger commercial studios added colour
on a production-line basis, with a
different artist adding each separate
colour, thereby increasing speed and
profitability. John Mayall capitalised on
the demand for coloured cartes by
offering his popular range of portraits of
the royal family coloured as well as
untinted. Colouring of somewhat poorer
quality is evident on many European cartes depicting traditional and regional
costumes, and widely produced for the tourist market.

Despite the rigid adherence to artistic conventions, the carte-de-visite was
not devoid of humour and, from the 1870s, a demand was created for comic
portraits which clearly and quite deliberately overturned the established
conventions of portraiture. While these may be, in part, an attempt to poke
gentle fun at the rigid constraints imposed on portraiture, there is no doubt that
they also offered a whole new range of cartes to a public already sated on a diet
of celebrities and royalty.

A variation on the theme of portraiture was presented by sportsmen.
Membership of a team – whether at school or otherwise – could well warrant a
visit to the studio. Individuals were generally posed as if having a normal
portrait taken, except that their props were the equipment used in their sport.
Teams presented a greater challenge and were more commonly photographed
outdoors. Cartes depicting school and university teams are relatively common
but national sporting teams are rare. One example is the carte-de-visite taken to
commemorate the first England cricket team to visit Australia in the 1860s. On
occasion, accomplished musicians would choose to be photographed with their
instruments although these images are unusual today.

Celebrity cartes

Although the photographic portraits might have been deeply entrenched in the artistic conventions of an earlier age, technical improvements in cameras and developing processes meant that photographs were now within the grasp of almost everyone. Writing in *The Atlantic Monthly* (1862), Oliver Wendell Holmes observed,

> Card portraits have become the social currency, the 'green-backs' of civilisation. The sitters who throng to the photographers' establishments are a curious study. They are of all ages, from the babe in arms to the old, wrinkled patriarchs and dames whose smiles have as many furrows as an ancient elm has rings.

But it was not only the poor who flocked to have their portraits taken. For the first time ordinary people could see, and possess, photographic images of their heroes and heroines, be they royalty or religious persons, actors or actresses, writers, politicians, military figures or simply people who had achieved notoriety through deed or deformity. William Darrah, writing in 1981, suggested that the huge trade in celebrity cartes was a reflection of the high level of 'commerce, colonisation, migrations of people, the missionary movement and accelerated communication.' To this list can also be added greater access to education, which encouraged eager minds to broaden their horizons.

A quaint, and widely accepted, story credits the beginnings of celebrity

Die Jeri & C⁰ᵉ Phot

cartes to a portrait of Napoleon III by André Adolphe Eugène Disdéri. Napoleon III is supposed to have passed Disdéri's Paris studio on the Boulevard des Italiens while marching at the head of his troops bound for Italy in 1859. On seeing the studio, he supposedly left the marching columns in order to have his picture taken. Although this story has now been discredited by recent research (which demonstrated that the troops did not march down the Boulevard des Italiens at all), there

Although the studio of Adolphe Disdéri was in Paris, Disdéri's reputation attracted many titled sitters from around the world. This portrait, dated 1862, shows the eighth Earl of Elgin shortly before his death in 1863. Born in 1811, he succeeded to the title in 1841 on the death of his father, who is best known for bringing the 'Elgin Marbles' from Greece to London in 1816. Between 1847 and 1856 the eighth Earl served as Governor-General of Canada. In 1857–8 he led an expedition to China and he became the second Viceroy of India in 1862, but he died after only a year in office.

is no doubt that Disdéri did photograph Napoleon III and his family in 1859 and that the portraits proved extremely popular. The *Photographic News* of 4th October 1861 reported that 'One Parisian portraitist [Disdéri] we are assured is at present not taking less than £48,000 a year'. Such success makes Disdéri's lonely death, in 1889, as a destitute in a Paris asylum even more tragic.

Interest in carte collecting was given a massive boost by a series of portraits of the royal family commissioned by Queen Victoria (herself an avid enthusiast and collector of cartes) from John Mayall of London in August 1860. Sixty thousand sets of Mayall's royal portraits were produced. These early portraits proved so popular that, over the next few years, Mayall earned a royalty of £35,000 from A. Marion & Company and was soon earning an income of £12,000 a year. Mayall's studio is said to have had an output of over 500,000 cartes annually while cartomania was at its peak.

THE EMPEROR NAPOLEON III
W. & D. DOWNEY   COPYRIGHT

Left: Commissions from Queen Victoria at Balmoral gave royal patronage to the firm of W. & D. Downey of Newcastle, and later London. In this portrait, from the late 1860s, Napoleon III of France appears rather more pensive than in his earlier portraits. Within a few years, France would be defeated in the Franco-Prussian War of 1870 and Napoleon's Second Empire would fall with his capture by the Prussians at Sedan only six weeks after the declaration of war. Exiled to Britain, Napoleon III died in 1873.

Right: Princess Alexandra, Princess of Wales, soon became a clear favourite of the British people and there were many different portraits available. This unusual portrait on a black background was taken by Rudolph Stiegler and published by Frederick Jones of London. Stiegler also produced the same portrait (which was widely pirated) on a cream background.

The scale of sales of celebrity cartes was truly astonishing. The *Photographic News* of 27th February 1885 suggests that the most popular carte (selling over 300,000 copies) was taken by W. & D. Downey in 1867, showing the Princess of Wales carrying her young daughter on her back. The same article states that Downey's 'photographed nearly every living crowned head of Europe, three Sultans of Turkey, two Emperors of Russia and the whole English Royal Family down to Prince Henry of Battenberg'.

The untimely death from typhoid of Prince Albert, the Prince Consort, in December 1861 led to a rush on cartes depicting him. Some seventy thousand were reported to have been ordered from the publishing wholesale company A. Marion & Company in just one week. There would also have been many thousands of pirated copies. Sympathy for the bereaved Queen manifested itself in the purchase of Mayall's portraits, which were being ordered 'by the

Despite being spotted by imperfections in the photographic paper, this portrait of Prince Albert, the Prince Consort, by John Mayall of London captures the character of the man. Although never taken to heart by many of the British people, Albert worked tirelessly on their behalf right up to his death from typhoid in 1861. This carte was produced in 1867, demonstrating the demand for his image.

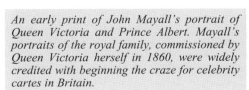

An early print of John Mayall's portrait of Queen Victoria and Prince Albert. Mayall's portraits of the royal family, commissioned by Queen Victoria herself in 1860, were widely credited with beginning the craze for celebrity cartes in Britain.

THE QUEEN & PRINCE CONSORT

100,000', according to the *Photographic News* of 28th February 1862 – a huge demonstration of public support.

Queen Victoria acquired her interest in photography from Prince Albert, who had built a darkroom within Windsor Castle and frequently bestowed commissions upon photographers such as Roger Fenton. Comparing Prince Albert's interest with that of Queen Victoria, Alan Thomas (writing in 1978) suggests that 'Queen Victoria's interest was less enlightened: possessed of a strongly literal cast of mind, she appears to have employed the new medium as a means of grasping hold of the material world.' To achieve this, the Queen ardently collected cartes, building up a formidable collection filling thirty-six albums. The Honourable Eleanor Stanley (one of the Queen's ladies-in-waiting) wrote on 24th November 1860, 'I have been writing to all the fine ladies in London for their and their husbands' photographs, for the Queen. I believe the Queen could be bought and sold for a photograph.'

Queen Victoria was not the only royal person to collect cartes. Empress Elisabeth of Austria began a collection of female beauties in March 1862. Her requests for additions to her collection were sent by the Austrian foreign minister to Austrian embassies throughout the world. The Sultan of Turkey had a harem

Otto von Bismarck (1815–98) remains a fascinating character in European history. After forty-seven years of liberal and nationalist failure to unite the states of the German Confederation, Bismarck took only nine years, completing the task with the clinically efficient defeat of France in the Franco-Prussian War of 1870. In recognition of his achievements, Bismarck was made a prince in 1871. Bismarck's subsequent career as Germany's first Chancellor was marred by a series of domestic conflicts which ultimately left him isolated. The young King William II eventually forced Bismarck to resign in 1890. This portrait was taken by Albert Mendelssohn of London, Berlin and Hamburg.

Albert Mendelssohn.   *London*

of some four hundred beautiful women who were highly valued and unapproachable, so it is a credit to the skills of the Austrian diplomats that the Empress Elisabeth's albums contain a number of portraits of these women.

The establishment of wholesale publishers was a reflection of the trade in celebrity cartes. Such companies gathered together negatives from private and commercial photographers, or commissioned their own, and used them to produce trade lists. Larger publishers issued catalogues listing the titles available. Many trade lists also included copies of photographs that had been shamelessly pirated. Indeed, pirating was a widespread practice. The vast majority of celebrity cartes with no backplates can be safely assumed to be pirate copies. Some photographers blatantly placed their own labels on to pirated photographs. William Darrah quotes two examples from the lists of American photographer Mathew Brady. Brady's carte of John Wilkes Booth (the assassin of President Abraham Lincoln) was copied from a portrait by Silsbee, Case & Company of Boston while his carte of Edgar Allan Poe came from a daguerreotype from the gallery of Masury & Hartshorn.

In order to encourage the famous to pose for their portraits, sitters were offered either a flat fee (determined by reference to their fame and therefore the likely popularity of the carte) or a royalty based on the number of cartes

Unlike most celebrities, who were prepared to accept a royalty from carte sales, the actress Sarah Bernhardt demanded a fee from photographer Sarony in return for her portrait, published in 1880. This carte has been pirated but retains most of the Sarony credits beneath the portrait.

sold. A. Marion & Company are reputed to have paid a royalty as high as £400 per ten thousand copies sold. Cartes of celebrities were known in the trade as 'sure cards' because of the almost certain profits to be made from them. Although few photographers established a trade list as large as that of Marion's, many claimed at least a few celebrities among their issues. However, in some cases simply being related to a celebrity was sufficient to justify being marketed oneself. The wife of Thomas Carlyle wrote to her husband:

> The great testimony to your fame seems to me to be the fact that my photograph is stuck up in Macmichael's window…It proves the interest, or curiosity, you excite; for being neither a 'distinguished authoress', nor a 'celebrated murderess', nor an actress…it can only be as Mrs Carlyle that they offer me.

Some celebrities, like the actress Sarah Bernhardt, charged the photographer for the privilege of taking their portrait. Miss Bernhardt is reputed to have charged Napoleon Sarony several hundred dollars for the right to publish her carte while on a visit to New York in the late 1870s. The price was certainly worth paying. The opportunity to photograph a celebrity (and especially a member of the royal family) gave a studio the distinction of favoured patronage which they eagerly exploited on the backplates of their products. Ridiculously large numbers of British photographers boasted royal patronage. The studio of Henry Peach Robinson could legitimately boast of being 'Patronised by Her Majesty', as could Hills & Saunders of London. However, the claim of G. Churchill of Eastbourne to be 'Photographer to her Majesty the Queen and most of the Imperial and Royal families of Europe' must be treated with a little scepticism! The practice of encouraging distinguished patronage was not unique to Britain, however: Francis Chit of Bangkok advertised himself as 'Photographer to the King of Siam'.

The motivation for politicians to have their portraits circulated is obvious, the more exposure politicians get, the more likely they are to capture the imagination (and therefore the support) of the populace. Carte sales provided an excellent barometer of current popularity. Lord Brougham, on passing a shop window displaying his carte, would always enquire as to how it was selling.

Not all distinguished sitters were enthusiastic about it, however. W. & D. Downey (then of Newcastle) were commissioned annually by Queen Victoria to photograph guests at her Balmoral estate. One year, having completed their

Charles Dickens was one of Britain's best-loved authors in the nineteenth century, and his work is still widely read today. Indeed, many of the established images of Victorian London owe more to his writing than to any other source. The signature, although that of Dickens, was printed on to the card. This portrait was produced by the London Stereoscopic and Photographic Company, c.1862. The reverse of the carte advertises medals won by the company in London, Berlin, Dublin and New York and announces that the company were 'Sole Photographers to the International Exhibition 1862'.

task and set off on holiday, they were recalled to Balmoral to photograph Benjamin Disraeli, the leader of the Conservative Party, who had just arrived. Disraeli was a far-from-willing sitter. On two successive days the sittings were unsuccessful – on one day because Disraeli was nervous about the effects of impending rain on his velvet jacket. One of the Queen's ladies-in-waiting persuaded Disraeli to try once more and he agreed to sit for no more than five minutes – in the same velvet jacket! The portrait obtained from this sitting went on to sell thousands of copies during Disraeli's second term as prime minister (1874–80). William Downey also photographed a number of the Pre-Raphaelite circle including Dante Gabriel Rossetti, John Ruskin, Arthur Hughes and William Bell Scott. On 29th June 1863, Ruskin was photographed with Rossetti and Scott. When the resulting photograph was later published, Ruskin denounced Downey as 'a mere blackguard'! The actress Sarah Bernhardt was rather more positive in her views as expressed in Downey's autograph book: *'Vous êtes le plus aimable des hommes, et le roi des photographs...je crie, Vive le roi Downey.'* ('You are the dearest of men, and the king of photographs... I cry "Long live King Downey."')

A fine vignetted portrait of Benjamin Disraeli (1804–81) by H. Lenthall (successor to Mr Kilburn) of Regent Street, London, c.1864. Disraeli began his political career as MP for Maidstone in 1837. By 1852 he was Chancellor of the Exchequer and later Leader of the House of Commons. In 1868 he became Prime Minister for ten months, and he held the post again between 1874 and 1880.

In the United States, the explosion of interest in celebrity cartes coincided with the outbreak of the Civil War (1861–5). Military and political leaders on both sides of the conflict were widely photographed – their popularity extending across the Atlantic. Many British carte-de-visite albums contain portraits of leading American figures, reflecting the private allegiances of the household. So popular were cartes-de-visite that the United States government decided to tax them as a means of raising money to finance the war. Between August 1864 and August 1866 the law required that a tax stamp be attached to the back of every carte. The studio or other seller would then cancel the stamp at the time of purchase. The denomination of stamp was directly related to the cost of the photograph: 2 cents for cartes costing less than 25 cents, 3 cents for those costing between 25 and 50 cents, and 5 cents for every additional dollar. Many different types and colours of stamp were used. The blue 2 cent 'playing cards' stamp, however, was used only in the summer of 1866 and is therefore especially useful for precise dating. Occasionally the cancellation may include a specific date although a stroke of the pen or a signature is more common. Although the United States government was the only one to impose a tax on photography, it was certainly not the only one to consider it. The British government debated the idea on several occasions. As prime minister, W. E. Gladstone considered a penny tax in 1864, as did Benjamin Disraeli in 1868, when it was calculated that a tax of one penny on the approximately five million cartes being sold annually in Britain would bring in sufficient revenue to finance the war in Abyssinia. None of these proposals ever materialised, possibly, as Helmut Gernsheim suggests, owing to the intervention of Queen Victoria, who was reluctant to tax the pleasures of the poor.

In the late 1860s and 1870s, the emphasis shifted from an interest

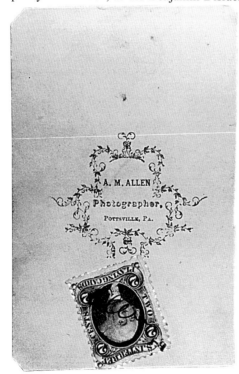

This carte, by A. M. Allen of Pottsville, Pennsylvania, bears the rare blue 'playing cards' revenue stamp, which was used only during the summer of 1866. The stamp has been cancelled by the photographer, or a member of his staff, writing 'Allen' across the face. The corners of this carte have been cut off in order to facilitate slipping the carte into the sleeves of an album.

Portraits of people with unusual attributes (height, weight, etc) became popular in the late 1860s and well into the 1870s. This composite portrait shows John Harris and his family. Harris was born in 1815 in Cardiganshire. He reached the height of 44.5 inches (113 cm) and weighed 65 pounds (29.5 kg). By comparison, his wife Margaret was 65 inches (165 cm) in height and weighed 195 pounds (88.5 kg).

in celebrities towards cartes depicting individuals famed for their notoriety or appearance. The Americans embraced this trend rather more enthusiastically than the Europeans. The most prolific American producer of such cartes was Charles Eisenmann of New York, who listed more than two thousand portraits, including fat or bearded ladies, human skeletons (unusually thin people), dwarves, giants, people lacking limbs, Siamese twins and many others, often drawn from travelling shows or circuses. One presumes that the income generated by the publicity was the motivation for the sitters in the years before they could claim any state aid to alleviate their suffering.

Even long-dead celebrities were fair game for the rapidly expanding trade lists. The American photographer Mathew Brady raided his archive

GEN. TOM THUMB, WIFE & CHILD.

General Tom Thumb (real name Charles Stratton), an American midget showman, and his wife, Lavinia Warren Stratton, were popular subjects for carte portraits. This carte (with a 'borrowed' baby, since they had no children) has no photographer's imprint and may therefore be pirated. Tom Thumb's wedding portraits were taken by Mathew Brady and published by E. & A. T. Anthony. Many of these wedding portraits were issued with the bride's and groom's signatures printed on the card mount.

of daguerreotypes of famous people in order to reissue them in the carte format. Cartes copied from paintings and engravings proved equally popular with collectors, and portraits of Renaissance artists sat side by side with other famous characters from history. As William Darrah observes, these cartes provided the basis for illustrations for almost all encyclopedic texts published between 1880 and 1915.

An unusual variation on the celebrity theme was the montage. First appearing in the 1860s, these continued throughout the period of the cartes. Disdéri obtained a French patent for carte montages in 1863 but he could not claim to have invented the process, which involved producing an image from a number of prints cut out and arranged in a design. Almost any group of people, from royalty and politicians, to religious figures, was presented in this format. Some

All manner of people were photographed during the peak of carte collection in the mid 1860s. This portrait, by J. Flament of Brussels, shows a gentleman pointing to a still very alert head 'placed' on an adjacent table. Presumably the viewer is not meant to notice the crossed legs beneath the table.

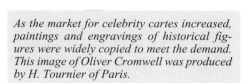

As the market for celebrity cartes increased, paintings and engravings of historical figures were widely copied to meet the demand. This image of Oliver Cromwell was produced by H. Tournier of Paris.

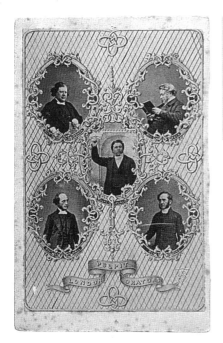

Composite photographs were popular with many photographers and were used to depict a wide range of subjects from clergymen to musicians. The composite format was also used to produce various souvenirs of holiday destinations – the forerunner of the modern picture postcard. This carte portrays the leading London pulpit orators and dates from the mid to late 1860s.

There were no limits to the new gimmicks employed to sell cartes. Composite images of five hundred or even one thousand identifiable figures were available. The portraits on this carte include people (contemporary and historical) from all parts of the globe and (with some prominence) leading figures from both sides of the American Civil War.

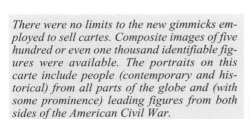

of the most ambitious versions boasted between five hundred and a thousand recognisable portraits on one carte. One distributed by F. J. Roberts of Euston Square, London, advertised 'Upwards of five hundred photographic portraits of the most celebrated personages of the age'. Not to be outdone, however, the 'Great Sensation Card' (published by Ashford Brothers & Company, 76 Newgate Street, London) devoted most of its reverse side to extolling its virtues.

This extraordinary production of modern art contains the portraits of over 1,000 living and historical celebrities and is designed not merely as a photographic curiosity but as a medium of instruction and entertainment. The publishers believe it impossible for anyone to glance over it without at once recognising the portraits of very many whose deeds are as familiar as household words, thereby introducing an easy and agreeable source of conversation into all circles of society.

Photographing the cycle of life

The bulky panoply of photography was inappropriate at the moment of birth but, as soon as was practicable, parents were keen to obtain a photographic record of their offspring. Although it posed many difficulties, photographers were keen to encourage this trade since other family members could also be enticed to have their portraits taken, either at the time or at later sittings. The family could also be encouraged to return at regular intervals to record the child's development.

The difficulties for the photographer lay in adapting a distracted and uninterested young child to the rigorous physical demands imposed by portrait photography. Although the exposure time had been reduced to mere seconds, it was still asking a lot of any baby to remain motionless, let alone affect a pleasing expression! If the photographer was to avoid working his camera at a very low level, it was necessary to elevate the child by placing it in a chair or other similar item of furniture. Once up there, the child had to be secured in place and encouraged to be photogenic. The problem was often compounded by the fact that the child was generally accompanied by a retinue of adults which might include parents, grandparents, other relatives and, in richer families, the nurse. With each person

Photographing very young children posed many problems for the portrait photographer. Here the all-too-typical white gown would have demanded considerable skill from the photographer. Since the clothing would have required less exposure time than the face it was necessary to mask parts of the image in order to avoid loss of detail. There was also the risk that a child would move and cause the image to blur. In this portrait, by H. Lenthall (successor to Mr Kilburn) of Regent Street, London, the child is perched on a cushion and restrained – probably by the tartan sash, which would have been tied around the back of the chair.

likely to offer his or her own advice on how the child should be posed and entertained, the photographer's autonomy was seriously challenged. A number of photographers went so far as to ban parents from the room. As if such distractions were not enough, young children were often presented dressed in white linen, which created a number of technical difficulties for the photographer, in that the hands and face would require longer exposure than the clothing.

Once the child was posed, he or she had to be persuaded to hold the pose. Older children could be supported by items of furniture or head-clamps but younger children and babies presented greater problems. Decorative sashes or scarves could be extended around the back of the chair to tie the child in place or, equally commonly, an adult could be concealed behind the chair to hold the child still. The parent's hands could be hidden underneath carefully draped fabric but they are visible in many photographs. Occasionally the adults themselves can be seen although they are often largely removed by vignetting. A very young child could be seated on the mother's lap and this remained a common pose, echoing the popular image of the Madonna and Child. More rarely, young children

Above left: W. Haddy of Brixham, Devon, took this portrait of 'Master Barnes'. Supported by a chair on one side and a neck clamp behind him, this child was kept firmly in place. A larger neck clamp for adults can be seen behind the boy.

Above right: This child's expression suggests a degree of frustration, which could explain the presence of an adult (possibly the child's mother) partly concealed behind the chair, holding the child in place.

might be photographed in their prams and outdoor clothing.

Children were often posed with toys, which also served as a distraction for them. However, these were normally expensive studio props intended to suggest wealth rather than simply for play, and they could cause blurring of the image if moved. Such props might include dolls, prams and toy drums. Older boys might be posed holding a whip, drum or toy rifle whereas girls held dolls or baskets. Noisier toys were often used by the photographer or an assistant to attract and hold the child's attention during the exposure of the plate. Despite the best efforts of the photographers, children did often prove harder to photograph than older sitters and, in consequence, the process took longer and wasted more plates. A number of photographers charged more for children and a few refused to photograph them at all. Cartes produced by H. Wilcox merely stated that prices would be agreed for 'large portraits, groups and children'.

Louis KETTLE

M⁇⁇ WILLIAMS.   PHOTO.

Above: *Young Louis Kettle cuts a dashing figure as he poses atop this splendid dappled rocking horse. To complete the equestrian theme, Louis also carries a riding crop (a common accessory in portraits of young boys).*

Left: *A series of cartes by John Mayall of London depicting Queen Victoria's young sons Arthur and Leopold in Scottish dress led to a new fashion craze. This child, portrayed by Walter Hildyard of Manchester, wears clothing clearly showing Scottish influence. To assist the child hold the pose, he rests one arm on the back of the chair while the other arm is locked in place by tucking the thumb into a pocket. The biggest risk remaining would appear to be the danger of the child's weight causing the chair to topple backwards!*

Appleton & Company of Bradford took this charming portrait of a young child in the late 1870s. Unusually, the child remains dressed in outdoor clothing (carefully arranged to emphasise the elaborate decoration) and the pushchair serves to hold the child's pose. The retractable sun canopy and waterproof cover can clearly be seen.

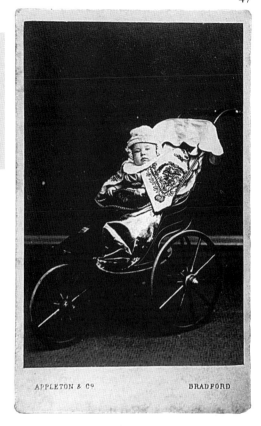

APPLETON & Cº   BRADFORD

The commercial photographer's nightmare must have been a commission to photograph a young child with his or her favourite pet. Pets (most commonly dogs and horses) were even less inclined to hold a pose than the children, and a twitching tail or ear could ruin a sitting.

Children would also be photographed at key stages in their growth and achievement – for example the time when the skirts worn by the youngest children were changed for the short trousers worn by older ones. Acquisition of a school uniform, or membership of a club or society, could also be cause for celebration. For wealthier families, the first day at public school could warrant a visit to the photographic studio. Poorer families tended not to record the beginnings of formal education (which often did not exist until the mid 1870s) but class photographs were common. The children would be posed in rows accompanied by their class teacher and the headmaster. Often a school slate would be inscribed with the details of the class and the occasion. At a time when school funding was very closely linked to attendance and achievement, photographs were often taken of children who had achieved full attendance for the term.

School groups were often photographed to record students achieving academic success or with excellent records of attendance. Throughout the nineteenth century, children were generally segregated. This photograph shows Standard 4 of one girls' school as shown on the slate held by the girl nearest to the camera. Many of these portraits were taken by itinerant photographers and therefore have no studio imprints. This image was taken c.1880.

The upright pose and neat appearance attest the pride and self-respect of the subjects in this carte showing the Stockwell Orphanage Handbell Ringers c.1890, by William Mountain of London. The unusual theme of this group portrait and the details of provenance make images like this very collectible.

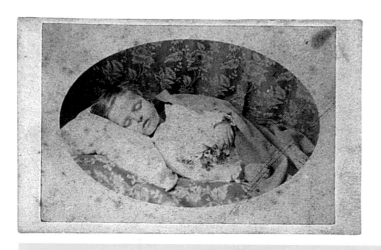

An unidentified photographer took this post-mortem carte of a young girl posed as if in sleep. The positioning of the bedcover and the small bouquet of flowers in her hand help confirm that the child is dead. Unusually the child is laid on material, decorated with flowers, which has been raised up behind her to provide an appropriate backdrop. The carte dates from c.1870.

Medical advances in the nineteenth century were not sufficient to reduce substantially the high infant mortality rate. Sometimes, children succumbed to 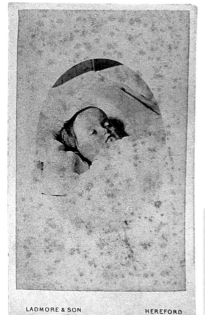 illness even before their first visit to the photographer's studio. To preserve the memory, post-mortem portraits were taken with the child's body posed as in sleep. William Darrah notes an image bearing the inscription 'taken while dying'. On rare occasions, the dead child was held in the mother's arms. Although such images may appear macabre today, in the nineteenth century they offered a tangible and comforting reminder of a lost child, who deserved to appear alongside siblings and other relatives in the family album. The death of a child was a constant threat and the object of a number of carte issues depicting reassuring

LADMORE & SON   HEREFORD

Ladmore & Son of Hereford photographed this young child in death c.1875. The child is again posed as if asleep but the inscription on the reverse of the carte identifies it as a post-mortem portrait (although the child is not named). With a child of this age, a post-mortem photograph such as this might have been the only portrait taken.

A painting specially commissioned for the carte-de-visite format. Many versions of this image appear and it was widely distributed. One copy, entitled 'To God', produced by W. V. Kaulbach as number 125 in a series, had the title printed in three languages, reflecting its wide circulation. Another version of the same picture bears the title 'Angel and Flowers' — apparently ignoring the significance of the child in the angel's arms.

images of angels collecting the departing spirits of dead infants. Whilst appearing mawkishly sentimental to modern eyes, these cartes must have offered some comfort to the bereaved, who were able to visualise their child's salvation.

Children of the wealthy who went on to further education were often photographed on the occasion of their graduation from university wearing the robes that signified their achievement. For those whose education was more elementary the completion of an apprenticeship was an occasion of equal pride. The sitter would be shown bearing the tools and accoutrements appropriate to the trade.

An engagement or wedding would certainly merit the photographer's attention. The image of the traditional 'white wedding' is a largely twentieth-century one – white wedding dresses were not commonly worn by the lower social classes, for whom the normal attire for a bride was her best formal dress, which could also continue in service for attendance at church on Sundays and public holidays. White dresses were also extremely difficult to photograph since the bride's face and hands would need rather more exposure time than the dress, leading to the

The Cambridge branch of Hills & Saunders took this portrait of a young man in his academic robes, c.1870. He has either recently graduated or secured a teaching appointment and this portrait was taken to commemorate the event.

HILLS & SAUNDERS · CAMBRIDGE & OXFORD
ALSO AT ETON HARROW & LONDON

Brides in white were becoming more numerous by the early 1870s but remained a minority for most of the century. This bride (identified only as 'Corrie, the youngest, in her bridal dress') has been carefully posed to show off her engagement and wedding rings. A number of fingerprints can be seen on the image; they are probably the result of handling during development.

J. Joyner of High Street, Chel-tenham, took this portrait of an unidentified couple. The man is seated, holding a book to em-phasise his literary skills, while his wife rests her hand on his shoulder. The careful position-ing of the lady's hands to show off her ring finger may suggest that this is a wedding portrait.

effect known as 'burn-out' (where all detail of the dress is lost).

Once in the studio, the engaged or married couple were treated in the same way as any other sitters. This makes the identification of such photographs very difficult. Audrey Linkman observes that there was often little or no physical contact between the engaged couple and the only clue is therefore the prominence given to the ring finger. A little more contact was appropriate between married sitters. The husband was generally seated, with his wife standing with her hand resting on his shoulder. By the late 1880s, this pose was seen as the hallmark of photographs of married or engaged couples and Linkman suggests that other couples, not formally engaged or married, who chose to be photographed in this pose laid themselves open to criticism. For the photographer, the advantage of having the gentleman seated was that it brought both parties into sharper focus; this would be rather more difficult if the man (often taller) was posed standing.

In the 1860s and 1870s, the studio portrait of the bridal couple was often the only photographic record of the event since additional photographs of the guests and officiating clergy involved further expense that made it impractical. In the early 1870s, some commercial photographers began to make copies of marriage announcements in *The Times*. These photographs – in carte-de-visite format – were then mailed to those mentioned, with the request that the photographer be reimbursed or the photographs returned.

In addition to recording engagements and marriages, photographs would be taken upon entry into a profession, the receipt of promotion at work or other noteworthy achievement. Many commercial photographers established their studios in close proximity to military or naval bases and relied on such custom for a sizeable proportion of their incomes, as evidenced by the expenses incurred in providing appropriate nautical or military backdrops. A new entrant to the

Left: An extract from 'The Times' dated 25th February 1882 detailing recent marriages. Such cartes were produced and circulated to those mentioned in the hope that they might wish to purchase a copy. This carte was produced by Marc Hughes of Hammersmith, London, who marketed his products as a 'Souvenir de Temps'.

A career in the Navy was the ambition of many young men. This young sailor, photographed by A. Reeves of Plymouth in the mid 1860s, was clearly proud of his achievements. The painted backdrop shows small boats at sea as seen through a window, the frame of which is also painted.

The pronounced crease across the upper thigh of this soldier's trousers suggests that the uniform is still rather new and that the portrait might be intended to celebrate his acceptance into the élite French light infantry. Although the painted backdrop depicts the Colosseum in Rome, the soldier is probably French. The soldiers of regiments that wore uniforms like this were known as Zouaves. This image dates from c.1870 and was found in an album with a number of cartes showing scenes from the Franco-Prussian War.

legal or academic profession or the clergy might justify a sitting in full professional attire. A relatively small number of working-class artisans, taking equal pride in their achievements, chose to be photographed in their everyday work clothes and bearing the tools of their trade. People in service, building labourers and other workers immediately sacrificed any pretence at higher social status by being photographed in this way but their portraits clearly reflect their pride in their own success. (The widely distributed cartes of coastal fisherwomen and characters in traditional regional dress do not fit into this category since they were produced largely to satisfy the developing thirst for tourist souvenirs.)

An unusual portrait depicting a fireman of the Brighton Volunteer Fire Brigade (as shown by the letters on his cap). His axe is holstered and given prominence in this carte by W. & A. H. Fry of Brighton, dating to the early 1870s. Note also the crossed axes insignia worn on his collar.

W.& A. H. FRY, PHOTOS.   BRIGHTON

Thomas Rowe of Exeter took this portrait of two young stonemasons (possibly brothers from their resemblance) posed against a rough stone wall, c.1890. Bearing the tools of their trade, these men give the impression of having come straight from work. The portrait may have been taken to commemorate the completion of an apprenticeship.

Just as the photographer would be called upon to record the beginnings of a new life, so too would he have a role at the end of a life. The funeral and subsequent erection of an appropriate memorial were highly expensive social necessities. Getting the details right – and satisfying the expectations of family and friends – was a task capable of devastating a family's finances. As early as 1843, the reformer Edwin Chadwick (whose reports on the conditions of the working people of Great Britain eventually led to the 1848 Public Health Act) noted that the funeral of a 'gentleman' could cost between £150 and £1000; that of a lawyer or similar could cost £100; someone of 'moderate respectability' could be buried for £60 while a 'tradesman of better class' could expect to pay £50 – all substantial amounts of money in those days. The photographer would be expected to produce a suitable memorial image for distribution to mourners. Often this would require him to look back through his negative archive and reprint suitable images of the deceased, presenting them on specially printed cards commonly edged in black and bearing

A memorial carte by John Cann of Tiverton, Devon. The black border and memorial in-scription ('His sun is gone down while it was yet day') were already prepared and placed over an existing portrait of the deceased from the photographer's negative archive. The portrait and frame were then photographed together, which explains the loss of definition on the inscription. The deceased was usually referred to by name with details of the date of death and often the burial.

Edmund Baker of Birmingham took this photograph showing the memorial to William Henry Morrish Heal, who died in 1882 aged twenty-one. The inscription beneath the dedication notes that the memorial was erected by his friends – a clear testament to his popularity. The material beneath and behind the tablet shows that the photograph was taken prior to the erection of the memorial.

the details of the deceased. The photographer would also record the grave itself to show relatives and friends unable to attend the funeral that an appropriate memorial had been erected. Great care was taken with these photographs to try and present the grave as being isolated from others (suggesting greater expense and importance). This could be done by careful positioning which would leave adjoining graves out of the frame. On occasion, the photographer would be called upon to photograph the deceased person. This practice was sanctioned at the highest level – Queen Victoria commissioned a portrait of Prince Albert on his deathbed which she had framed and kept on the wall of the bedroom. Today, the majority of surviving post-mortem portraits are of children but it would be wrong to think that they were the only subjects.

Some photographers capitalised on the Victorian fascination with death by claiming to be able to photograph the spirits of deceased loved ones. Although more reputable photographers criticised this practice and published details of how the deception could be achieved, and although the majority of these 'spirit' images were clearly faked, there remained a market for them.

Mr F. Balls of Ipswich photographed the grave of Jabez and Charlotte Mowle probably very soon after the interment of Jabez Mowle in 1872. By giving the monument such prominence in the photograph, the photographer conveys the impression that the grave is larger and more elaborate than those around it – a reassurance to family members unable to pay their respects in person.

Special occasions, events and places

Although the camera was still a long way from being able to record any major event as it occurred, the rapid spread of photography in the 1840s led the *National Gazette* of Philadelphia to proclaim (in terms which appear to herald the tabloid journalism of today): 'A steam boiler cannot explode, or an ambitious river overflow its banks – a gardener cannot elope with an heiress, or a reverend bishop commit an indiscretion, but straight away an officious daguerreotype will proclaim the whole affair to the world.' The ability to reproduce multiple copies in the carte-de-visite format brought such events – and indiscretions – to a far wider audience.

Thanks to the carte-de-visite, the expanding world was opened up in a way never previously thought possible. From now on, the expansion of the British Empire could be clearly chronicled and the wealth and diversity of culture of countries annexed to Britain brought into the drawing rooms of middle England. The second half of the nineteenth century was also a time of major political change in Europe. Both Italy and Germany had been united under charismatic and colourful leaders – Garibaldi and Cavour in Italy and Bismarck in Germany. While Italian unification had been achieved without widespread conflict, Bismarck's

Ashford Brothers & Company of London took and published this portrait of the Italian patriot Giuseppe Garibaldi (1807–82). Garibaldi sailed from Genoa in May 1860 with one thousand supporters to invade Naples and Sicily. Having defeated the Neapolitan army, he marched north and handed his conquests to the king of Piedmont, who was later proclaimed ruler of the newly united Italy. During the Franco-Prussian War of 1870, Garibaldi served with the French forces. Garibaldi captured the imagination of Victorian England – the epitome of the romantic patriot-leader.

Abraham Lincoln as photographed by Mathew Brady in a carte published by E. & A. T. Anthony of New York. Lincoln (1809–65) ran for the presidency of the United States in 1860 and won, largely because of splits in the Democrat party. His stance on slavery led to seven states seceding from the Union before Lincoln had even taken office in March 1861. He is best remembered as a champion of slave emancipation although slavery was not abolished until 1st January 1863. On 14th April 1865, one week after the surrender of the Confederate Army of Northern Virginia under General Robert E. Lee, Lincoln was shot by actor John Wilkes Booth. Lincoln died the next morning.

unification of Germany involved three wars in only six years – against Denmark in 1864, Austria in 1866 and France in 1870. The United States of America had also undergone major social and political upheavals in a civil war which cost the lives of over 600,000 Americans between 1861 and 1865. Although photographer Roger Fenton had extensively recorded the camps and characters of the Crimean War (1854–6), the photographers of the American Civil War (using both stereoscopic and carte-de-visite formats) were the first to depict the true horror of war. As the American writer Oliver Wendell Holmes said of the photographs produced, 'Let him who wishes to know what war is look at this series of illustrations. The wrecks of manhood thrown together in careless heaps, or ranged in ghostly rows for burial, were alive but yesterday.'

The first photographer to attempt to record the American Civil War was Mathew Brady. Using a pass signed by President Abraham Lincoln himself, Brady took his photographic wagon (known to the mystified Northern soldiers as the 'Whatsit Wagon') to the first major battle of the war at Manassas (also known as Bull Run) near Washington DC. Here the fledgling Union army was routed by raw Southern troops and for three days Brady and his wagon were lost in the chaos that ensued. Undaunted, Brady continued his work, which was soon widely available as both cartes-de-visite and stereo cards.

Brady was not alone. The Northern army of the Potomac alone issued passes to over three hundred photographers. The war brought undreamt-of opportunities for commercial photographers, some of whom gave up their studios to travel with the army in the field. In addition to chronicling the events of the war,

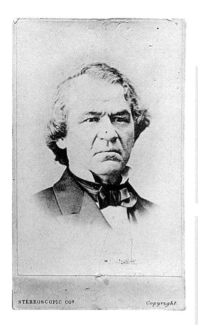

STEREOSCOPIC CO?   Copyright

Left: The London Stereoscopic and Photographic Company published this fine portrait of Lincoln's vice-president and successor, Andrew Johnson (1808–75). Born in North Carolina, Johnson became the only southern senator to support Lincoln. After Lincoln's assassination, Johnson attempted a conciliatory reconstruction policy. This led to his becoming the first American president to be impeached, although the impeachment eventually failed – by one vote.

Below: E. & A. T. Anthony of New York commissioned and published this carte of Confederate President Jefferson Davis (1808–89). Educated at West Point, Davis had served as Secretary of War under President Pierce (1853–7). Davis was given an extremely difficult task as president of the Confederacy but he remained in office despite increasing military reverses until captured in Georgia in May 1865. Subsequently imprisoned for two years, Davis was released and returned to his native Mississippi.

these photographers found that they had a captive market of homesick soldiers eager to send a carte-de-visite home to reassure loved ones of their continued good health.

On 17th September 1862 at Antietam, Alexander Gardner (a former employee of Brady who had left because of Brady's arrogant insistence on imprinting all photographs with his own name) took a series of pictures showing the true effects of the 'bloodiest day of the War'. Twenty-three thousand men were killed or wounded on that day and Gardner's photographs helped to reinforce the scale of the losses and, in the process, turn public opinion away from the maintenance of a conflict that seemed to have no end. Another former Brady employee, Timothy O'Sullivan, recorded some of the most emotive scenes of the war in the aftermath of the Battle of Gettysburg in July 1863. Although photographers were not present during the fighting they arrived within two days while

many of the dead were still unburied. Forty-three thousand men were killed or wounded in this epic struggle, which ended Confederate General Robert E. Lee's invasion of the North.

Alexander Gardner was with O'Sullivan at Gettysburg, where he took one of the best-known photographs of the American Civil War. Entitled 'Home of a Rebel Sharpshooter', it purported to show a dead Confederate sniper in a rocky outcrop known as 'the Devil's Den'. Whilst being an undeniably powerful and

General Robert E. Lee (1807–70) was a popular figure in British carte-de-visite albums. This portrait was published by C. D. Fredricks & Company of New York, Havana and Paris. As commander of the Confederate Army of Northern Virginia, Lee remains one of the best-known Confederate military leaders. After his defeat at Gettysburg, Pennsylvania, in 1863, Lee found himself increasingly on the defensive until his final surrender to General U. S. Grant at Appomatox Court House, Virginia, on 9th April 1865. Lee went on to become president of Washington College, Virginia.

Ordinary soldiers flocked to photographers' studios to have their 'likeness' taken. This portrait of Union Sergeant Samuel P. Martin was taken at the studio of Thomas J. Merritt in Nashville, Tennessee. He was a member of the Union force occupying Tennessee before the final Confederate collapse. He wears the standard-issue four-button sack coat and a fourteen-button high-collar military waistcoat (or 'vest').

evocative image, it also raised some of the earliest questions of ethics in photography, as it was faked. The soldier was simply an ordinary infantryman who had died some 40 metres away from the rocky outcrop. Gardner photographed the corpse in its original position and then moved the body and posed it for greater effect.

The impact of the war on families was reflected in the distribution of another carte, entitled 'Children of the Battlefield', which also touched America's

Collectors of cartes-de-visite are always keen to obtain identified images. This fine portrait of a Union officer is identified as 'Eli C. Merriam, 1st. Lieut. 1st. S.C. Vols.'. The first South Carolina Volunteer Regiment was the first regiment of ex-slaves raised to fight against the South. In common with all black regiments, the officers were white. The portrait was taken by Sam A. Cooley of Beaufort, South Carolina. This carte was found in a small album from the Shenandoah Valley, Virginia, along with a number of other portraits of Union officers.

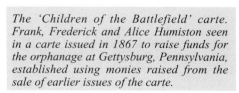

The 'Children of the Battlefield' carte. Frank, Frederick and Alice Humiston seen in a carte issued in 1867 to raise funds for the orphanage at Gettysburg, Pennsylvania, established using monies raised from the sale of earlier issues of the carte.

FRANK.   FREDERICK,   ALICE.

The sinking of the Confederate commerce raider 'Alabama' was a topic of considerable interest in Britain. Many of the crew were British and the ship had been built in the shipyards of Birkenhead. Although no photographs of the event were taken, naval artist Captain Anderson painted this dramatic reconstruction of events which was photographed and published by Frederic Jones of Oxford Street, London.

Another Confederate commerce raider built in Britain and having some British crew members was the 'Florida'. The 'Florida' undertook two cruises, the first under Captain John Newland Maffitt and the second under Lieutenant Charles Manigault Morris, who is shown in this portrait. In October 1864, the 'Florida' arrived at Bahia, Brazil, for repairs and refuelling. Soon after arrival, the ship was rammed by a United States warship while still in the harbour. The portraits of Morris and the other two officers were taken at the studio of João Goston in Bahia. The two officers are not identified on the carte but other photographs in the same album identify them as Thomas and Charles Comber. Initial searches of Confederate naval records have failed to find any reference to them.

Almost as soon as the American Civil War ended, the trade in relics and images of the war began. The firm of W. D. Selden & Company of Richmond, Virginia, advertised themselves as 'Dealers in Photographic Views, Confederate Relics, etc. of the Late War'. This carte, entitled 'The Heroes of Manassas', shows Generals Beauregard, Jackson and Johnson, Colonel Turner Ashby and President Davis at the first major battle of the Civil War.

social conscience. As the burial parties moved across the battlefield of Gettysburg, they came upon a corpse clutching a tintype showing three unidentified children. The original tintype was copied and widely distributed as cartes-de-visite in an attempt to identify the children. Eventually they were recognised as Frank, Frederick and Alice, whose father was Sergeant Humiston of the 154th New York Volunteer Regiment. Further copies of the picture were then published bearing the names of the children. The proceeds of this issue went towards the construction of an orphanage at Gettysburg, of which Sergeant Humiston's widow became the first matron. To reduce the risk of pirating, the carte bore a note pointing out that 'this picture is private property and can not be copied without wronging the Soldier's Orphans for whom it is published'.

The distribution of cartes depicting the terrible injuries inflicted upon slaves, most notably a much-copied image entitled 'The Scourged Back' which showed the effects of brutal lashings and was published by McAllister & Brothers, did much to focus the flagging Northern enthusiasm for the war. Similar results, though less dramatic, were achieved by issues of cartes showing freed slaves being educated in the North.

As the American Civil War was ending, Bismarck was extending Prussia's influence over the other states of the German confederation. In 1866, Prussian forces defeated Austria and effectively united the north German states. In an attempt to draw the Catholic southern states into the new Germany, Bismarck goaded the French government under Napoleon III into declaring war. The Prussians were able to mobilise one million men in only eighteen days. Using Germany's well-developed railway network, these men could be moved rapidly up to the front. French resistance was quickly swept aside and the French emperor himself captured. So quick was the German advance that few photographs were taken. Swiftly overrunning the forts surrounding Paris, the Prussian troops settled in for a four-month siege of the French capital. The people of Paris were soon reduced to starvation and eventually forced to surrender. The new German empire under Kaiser William of Prussia was proclaimed in the Great Hall of Mirrors in the Palace of Versailles. A number of carte issues were produced showing the damage caused by Prussian shelling, while others offered satirical comment on the Prussian success. Inevitably comparison was made between the leadership and capabilities of Napoleon III and the qualities of his more successful predecessor Napoleon Bonaparte, prompting renewed interest in images of Napoleon Bonaparte and the battlefield of Waterloo, scene of his final defeat in 1815.

In addition to recording scenes of war and their attendant messages, the carte-de-visite could also be used to prick the social conscience of a nation. However, in the same way that Gardner's photograph of the rebel sharpshooter at Gettysburg raised ethical questions, so too did the attempts of Thomas John Barnardo to draw the attention of the British public to the effects of poverty and homelessness among children. By 1874, there were estimated to be a staggering thirty thousand children sleeping rough in London – the capital of the richest nation on earth. Dr Barnardo used the carte-de-visite format to launch a social crusade. He opened a photographic unit in which he produced 'before' and 'after' portraits of the children rescued through his homes. These cartes were then sold to raise money for the maintenance of the children's homes. Critics accused Barnardo of artistic fiction, arguing that he tore the clothes of children to make them look more wretched than they actually were. Critics also pointed out that Barnardo's photograph of model Katie Smith as a match girl was misleading since, although she

BY WILL DIVINE MY DEAR AUGUSTA
WE'VE HAD ANOTHER AWFUL BUSTER
10,000 FRENCHMEN SENT BELOW
PRAISE GOD FROM WHOM ALL BLESSINGS FLOW

Britain remained neutral during the Franco-Prussian War of 1870 but increasing German militarism did begin to cause concern. This satirical cartoon pokes fun at the German successes. This carte was one of a series by W. O. Mason. It also bears the label of William Smith (Bookseller and Stationer) of London, who sold the carte at a price of one shilling.

Left: *This carte by the London Stereoscopic and Photographic Company purports to show a menu from the Siege of Paris in 1870.*

Siege Bread
Horse Soup
Dog Cutlets – aux petits pois
Ragout of Cat – à la Parisienne
Donkey – à la sauce soubise
Fricassee of Rats and Mice – à la Chinoise
Fillet of Mule – à la Portugaise
Roast Ostrich – à l'Allemande

This menu was apparently used at one of the last dinners given before the capitulation and was saved by Mr Washbourne of the United States Embassy.

Below: *Two portraits by Défossé of Paris showing Theodore Ellis and his grandfather. The annotation on Theodore's portrait shows that it was taken during the Siege of Paris in 1870. A number of other cartes relating to the siege were found in the same album. Theodore Ellis appears to wear a military uniform. His grandfather's sash seems to bear masonic insignia. Photography played an important part in the siege. Messages were photographed and, as microphotographs, attached to carrier pigeons, which flew in and out of Paris maintaining contact with the outside world.*

Traditional regional costumes were a popular subject for cartes-de-visite and were widely collected by Victorian travellers as souvenirs of their journeys. This portrait of an Italian gentleman was one of eight purchased on a tour which embraced Chiavari in northern Italy and Cagliari on the island of Sardinia. The cartes had been carefully chosen to reflect the full range of costumes – including a beggar. The identity of the photographer is unknown.

had had to work to survive, she had never been a match girl. Barnardo went to court to clear his name, arguing that it had been necessary to clean the children up as soon as they arrived because they were so filthy and therefore they had needed to be re-dressed for the 'before' pictures. Despite these arguments, Barnardo was found guilty of artistic fiction and his cause was consequently damaged.

However, although Barnardo's photographs were intended to protect children, many other photographers were prepared to exploit them. At a time when the age of consent was just thirteen, the poorest children could be exploited both commercially and sexually. The *Photographic News* of 1863 observed that 'a man who takes a walk with his wife and daughters dare not venture to look at the windows of our photographic publishers'. A decade later, a police raid on the Pimlico premises of photographer Henry Hayler seized 130,240 obscene photographs and 5,000 stereo cards.

Much of Britain's wealth was generated within the huge expanse of the British Empire, which eventually covered a quarter of the Earth's surface. The British public found more pleasure in viewing the expanding Empire than they did in confronting disturbing social issues at home. Today, the pyramids of

C. Portier of Algiers advertised 'vues et types de toutes l'Algérie'. His extensive range of cartes offers a fascinating insight into the lives of the Algerian people in the 1860s and 1870s. Here, nomadic tribesmen pose on their camels with their tents visible in the background.

TAKÉ NO OUCHI SHIMODZUKÉNO KAMI.
MATSUDAIRA IWAMINO KAMI.
KIOGOKU NOTONO KAMI.

The visit of Hiribourni Ito from Japan to Britain in 1863 was an important part of Japan's movement towards westernisation and aroused tremendous interest in the Japanese culture among the British people. This carte-de-visite, depicting three Samurai warriors, bears the backmark of Vernon Heath of London, but the image was sold by J. Haycraft (Bookseller, Printer and Stationer) of Manchester.

Egypt are known to almost everyone, but the first photographs of these and other monuments had an enormous impact on a public the majority of whom had never had the chance to travel beyond their home shores. Beyond the Empire, from the great plains of America in the west to the mysterious lands of China and Japan in the east, photographers were there to record the scenes and satisfy the increasing demand back home.

As railways made travel for the masses easier, the demand for views of popular tourist destinations increased. In Britain, most castles, cathedrals and other sites of historic interest were photographed and the views distributed as cartes-de-visite, as were many popular natural beauty spots and landmarks. The expansion of railways to the coast made the 'day at the seaside' a viable excursion for many working families in the last four decades of the nineteenth

Dating from the early 1870s, this carte of Eastbourne Pier by an unknown photographer reflects the increasing trend for holidays at the seaside. As young children paddle at the edge of the water, their parents watch from higher up the beach. The rapid movements of some of the children have caused the figures to become blurred despite the relatively short exposure time.

The distinctive costume of the coastal fisherwomen was a popular source of inspiration for local photographers. Sometimes the women were photographed against fishing boats in the local harbour, but studio portraits (often with appropriately painted backdrops and props) remain more common. In this carte-de-visite by W. Brooks of Penzance (dating from the late 1860s) a crab and a lobster serve to emphasise the women's trade.

century. Scenes of beaches, piers and bathing huts were widely produced, the forerunners of the picture postcards introduced in the 1880s. Another related source of photographic inspiration lay in the distinctive costume worn by the fisherwomen of these coastal areas. Studio photographs of women wearing these unusual costumes, or other distinctive regional dress, were widely available as souvenirs for tourists. Sometimes, well-placed hotels and inns would provide cartes depicting the premises with details of the proprietor and address, and more rarely the costs of food and accommodation, on the back.

In the United States, most communities were extensively recorded by local photographers in a way not replicated in Europe. Whereas European images concentrated on historic sites and structures and scenic vistas, American photographs reflected the nation's pride in its industrial and commercial achievements. Images abound showing mills, factories, banks, prisons, bridges and railway stations – the physical manifestations of progress and development. In Britain, there was an expanding market for cartes depicting the great churches and cathedrals. F. Bedford ('Photographer to H.R.H. The Prince of Wales') produced a large series of cartes depicting almost every aspect of Exeter Cathedral, inside and out. Exeter Cathedral was also the subject of at least one carte published by Provost & Company of Henrietta Street, Covent Garden, London.

This photograph by E. Goodfellow of Wincanton, Somerset, is typical of attempts to demonstrate the ability of photography to capture the smallest details with accuracy. The different shapes of the leaves on the trees provide contrast, as does the play of light on the stone wall behind the water trough.

Cartes-de-visite and art

The steady improvements in photographic equipment increasingly rendered outdoor photography practicable. The greatest asset of photography was its ability to reproduce even the smallest detail accurately. This immediately brought it into conflict with the Pre-Raphaelite Brotherhood of artists, who regarded

themselves as the only advocates of 'truth to nature'. The similar aims of the two media led to some public acrimony and much private collusion. Ford Madox Brown regularly talked with photographer Roger Fenton and for a time had been employed in a photographic studio; John Everett Millais relied on photographs to provide landscape backgrounds, while Dante Gabriel Rossetti photographed Jane Morris (wife of William Morris).

The photographer of this copyrighted image (dating from c.1865) is identified only by the initials 'S.P.' although the location (Fairlight Glen, near Hastings) is given in a large label stuck to the back of the mount. The photograph is clearly influenced by the Pre-Raphaelite movement. The view includes a wide variety of textures such as tree bark and branches, ivy-covered ground, exposed rocks and long grass in the foreground. The figures provide a scale but also encourage the viewer to ask questions about the image. Is the woman at the bottom hiding? If so, why?

Copyright .   S.P.

Above left: *F. S. Mann of Hastings took this beautiful study of a stream and waterfall surrounded by vegetation. The sun overhead brightly illuminates the tops of the leaves, providing a contrast with the darker vegetation beneath. It also serves to highlight the shapes of the different leaves – the ferns, the long blades of grass and smaller ivy leaves. The waterfall, with light playing on the water, provides a central focus and the large, moss-covered rocks encourage the eye to follow the stream down.*

Above right: *The angular shapes and textures of a scree slope below cliffs provided another good source of inspiration for Victorian photographers. This view of Weathercote, Yorkshire, was photographed by M. Horner and sold by Wildman & Son of Settle in the 1860s. The sunlight on the rocks exposes the cracks and fissures, which are further exaggerated by the growth of moss on some rock faces. The figures serve as a scale while the central waterfall provides a dramatic contrast with the angular rockface.*

The detail of rocks, leaves and running water proved an inspiration to photographers and artists alike. Improved cameras and reduced exposure times allowed photographers many more opportunities to move beyond the confines of the studio. They could now explore the potential of this new artistic medium and, at the same time, fuel the passion of a public eager to expand its horizons and retain a visual record of each hard-earned excursion to coast or countryside.

As the work of the Pre-Raphaelites became more fashionable, many photographers took up the challenge to show just how far photography was able 'to descend to the lowest details with undiminished attention' – the task given by Ruskin in 1855 to landscape painters. As a consequence, many carte-de-visite photographs appeared showing wooded glens, waterfalls and rocky outcrops. The *Photographic Journal* of 21st January 1857 observed that 'we have…boughs on which you may count the leaves, leaves on which you may

The ravages of ivy and other climbing plants were not widely appreciated in Victorian times and so many ancient and ruined structures were festooned with such plants, creating some very atmospheric views. J. V. Cobb of Hythe produced this carte of Saltwood Castle, Kent, in the late 1860s. The reverse of this image includes a potted history of the castle which was printed separately and glued on to the card.

Although the Pre-Raphaelites clearly influenced photography, the camera was also used to reproduce works by the Pre-Raphaelite artists. This carte, by an unidentified photographer, shows 'The Proscribed Royalist' by Millais, painted in 1853.

number the veins...'. A characteristic of such photographs, often presented in the carte-de-visite format, is the relative absence of sky. Many photographs concentrate on the natural details at such close range as to preclude sky altogether. When it does appear, it is generally confined to the periphery. Pre-Raphaelite pictures show very similar tendencies, demonstrating a clear bond between photography and art. The Victorian interest in romance encouraged the production of countless cartes-de-visite depicting castles and other ruined structures. The scale and majesty of the ruins fuelled interest in the history of the sites, while the texture of stones and vegetation appeased the artist's fascination for detail.

The Pre-Raphaelites were not the only ones to be influenced by or use photography. Edouard Manet's painting of 'The Execution of the Emperor Maximilian' (1868–9) relied on

As the demand for cartes increased, interest in classical art grew rapidly and some photographers specialised in photographing original works. This carte of Raphael's 'Madonna and Child' is by Gustav Schauer of Berlin and is numbered 188 in a series.

commercially available carte-de-visite portraits of the principal characters. The carte-de-visite could also bring established classical art into the drawing rooms of a public normally not given access to the great museums and art galleries of the world.

The Industrial Revolution created a new class in society and that new class demanded the rights of education previously held only by the landed gentry. This education included access to the world of classical art, and the carte-de-visite was the vehicle by which this access was to be achieved. As William Darrah so accurately observed,

> In less than ten years knowledge of the world's art treasures expanded from the exhibition halls of museums to the entire domain of western culture...How quickly Da Vinci's 'Mona Lisa', Raphael's 'Sistine Madonna', the 'Venus de Milo', the bust of Julius Caesar, the bronze of Romulus and Remus and the Wolf, and the 'Pieta' became familiar to millions, through the carte-de-visite.

Although many of these images were widely pirated, a number of publishers stand out, including Giocomo Brogi (who specialised in Italian masters) and the German firm of F. & O. Brockmann. Brockmann's series included an impressive range of contemporary art as well as established masterpieces. Often the notes on these cartes are given in several languages (commonly English, German and French), reflecting the international trade in such images. Gustav Schauer of Berlin imprinted many of his cartes of famous works of art with the label 'Photographic Art Publishing Institute, Berlin'.

Although these large publishing companies dominated the market, smaller photographers in almost every large town or city that had an art gallery produced cartes showing the best-known works of art held locally.

The interest in art was also extended to three-dimensional works of sculpture

Contemporary art was also the subject of attention. The International Exhibition of 1862 provided an excellent source of subjects for the London Stereoscopic and Photographic Company, who had sole rights to photograph the exhibition. This carte depicts 'L'Angeli dell Ariosto' by Macni.

L'ANGELI DELL ARIOSTO, BY MACNI.

International Exhibition. 1862.

and, by 1865, almost all important pieces had been photographed. The company of F. & O. Brockmann was also important in this trade. Sculpture associated with burials was also widely photographed although these images were generally commissioned by the family of the deceased rather than for wider commercial sale.

As the popularity of 'art' cartes increased, paintings and engravings were commissioned especially for the carte-de-visite format. Many of these commissioned works conveyed sentimental messages reflecting Victorian beliefs in the values of keeping busy, family love, obedience, learning, piety and kindness. Other images are humorous and intended simply to amuse. As variations on this theme, paintings and engravings were prepared which could be viewed in different ways, thereby communicating quite opposing messages. For example, one carte depicts two children playing under a bridge. However, viewed from a different angle, the arch of the bridge becomes a skull and the children's heads become the eye sockets. The carte is entitled 'Blossom and Decay'. Cartes depicting characters from stories such as Little Red Riding Hood were produced for the entertainment of the younger collector.

Comic, political and satirical cartoons can also be considered in this category. There is no limit to the range of subjects covered by these cartes. Some cartoons poked gentle fun at situations, for example a series of cartes depicting the adventures of 'Paddy' in Ireland by an unknown publisher and produced on very poor quality card stock. Others are rather more pointed: a carte commenting on the failed Fenian uprising shows a proud martial figure with the caption 'Going to War'; held upside down, the same figure becomes a donkey's head, with the caption 'Coming Home from War'.

The carte-de-visite in the home

Unlike daguerreotypes and ambrotypes, the carte-de-visite was produced primarily as an album photograph – in its earliest days it was referred to as 'the album portrait'. Despite the name 'carte-de-visite', very few photographers presented their images as visiting cards although occasional examples may be found.

When 'cartomania' flourished in the first half of the 1860s, purpose-designed albums were patented. The introduction of the carte-de-visite album further encouraged the spread and collection of images, and the more images were collected, the more profit was to be made by the commercial photographers.

The earliest albums were very similar to scrap books into which the unmounted cartes could be pasted. Often the images were then framed with pen and ink sketches. Later, albums were produced with pen-and-ink style illustrations already printed on to the pages. There was no limit to the range of subjects included in these albums. Popular topics included spring flowers, seashells, scenic views interspersed with small spaces for vignetted portraits, trailing ivy,

A page from an album in which the pages have been printed to look like hand-produced pen and ink artwork. In these albums, the unmounted cartes could be glued in to suit the taste of the owner. In this example, the figures of two men and a dog have been cut out and positioned to appear as part of the background.

A group of carte-de-visite albums ranging from the smallest containing only ten images to the largest containing a hundred and twenty (second from the left). The large album on the far left, a page from which is shown on page 74, was intended for unmounted images to be glued in rather than held in sleeves.

rope chains, autumn leaves, playing cards and suits, and ecclesiastical symbols. In the more expensive albums, each page would contain a different artwork. In an album from Kimbolton Castle (seat of the Duke of Manchester), the artworks bear the inscription 'Gowell's Anastic Press, Ipswich'. This album dates from the late 1870s but similar examples were produced well into the 1880s.

From the early 1860s, albums appeared with pages cut out to accommodate two cartes back-to-back in cardboard sleeves. These albums were made in a huge variety of shapes and styles to hold as few as eight and as many as one hundred images. The larger albums were popular with the photographers because empty pages encouraged further collecting in order to fill the blank spaces. Furthermore, when a carte was requested from a friend or relative, it was regarded as polite to return the favour. These albums did much to provide structure and formality to the craze of carte collecting.

The new albums were very carefully designed to reflect the external features of Bibles and prayer books, most notably the heavy leather bindings and metal clasps. Such measures suggested to the public that the photograph albums were worthy of the same awe and respect afforded to religious texts. Such embellishments also gave photography an image of luxury and prestige. It was doubtless hoped that the photograph album would take over the formal record of family history normally found on the front page of the family Bible. To combat this threat, some Bibles were even produced with slots for cartes-de-visite to be entered alongside the normal family details.

The first albums were produced for the French market and were introduced into Britain in 1860 and the United States shortly afterwards. Between 1861 and 1865, fifteen different patents were issued in the United States for carte albums. By 1867, one British firm alone claimed to have sold almost one million albums. The range and diversity of albums were impressive and included those specially designed to commemorate the dead. In the late 1880s, wedding albums were introduced with space beneath each image for an autograph.

In 1866, the larger 'cabinet' portrait was introduced by F. R. Window (who had pioneered the Diamond Cameo Portrait with rather less success in 1864) and immediately became popular. Both the carte-de-visite and cabinet formats co-existed until the end of the century and albums were produced with spaces to accommodate images in both formats. Manufacturers were always prepared to innovate and new shapes and gimmicks were constantly being introduced – semicircular albums, albums with musical boxes built into the back cover which played whenever the album was opened, and even albums with clocks built into the cover. The covers received the most attention from the manufacturers, being produced in a wide range of materials including leather, moulded thermoplastic, Japanese lacquer, wood and even mother-of-pearl.

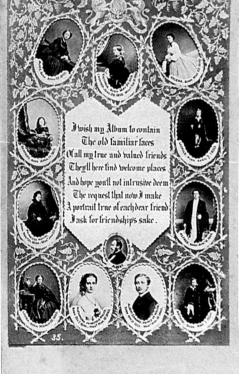

The first page of an album was commonly given over to an elaborate introductory carte which welcomed the viewer

A patriotic introductory carte depicting the members of the royal family c.1864. Although the photographer is unidentified, the clarity of the image suggests that this is not a pirated copy. Despite the royal theme, the rhyme was a common and widely used example.

Burgwitz & Company of Soho Square, London, produced this introductory album carte. Many different variations on the theme existed. In this example, ivy leaves have been placed around the framed rhyme, which is simply held up by the two girls.

and encouraged him or her to leave his own portrait. Many introductory cartes were available but some albums were sold with an introduction already in place which clearly emphasised the role of the album:

> Within this book your eyes may trace
> The well known smile on friendship's face;
> Here may your wondering eyes behold
> The friends of youth, the lov'd of old;
> And as you gaze with tearful eye,
> Sweet mem'ries of the years gone by
> Will come again with magic power,
> To charm the evening's pensive hour.
> Some in this book have passed the bourne
> From whence no travellers return;
> Some through the world yet doomed to roam,
> As pilgrims from their native home
> Are here by nature's power enshrined,
> As lov'd memorials to the mind –
> Till all shall reach that happy shore,
> Where friends and kindred part no more.

More colourful and elaborate introductory cartes often featured children or young ladies holding up a card bearing the introductory message, while others included composite images of the royal family or places of interest. A number of variations on the introductory message exist. The two most common versions read as follows:

> Yes, this is my album,
> But learn ere you look,
> That all are expected
> To add to my book.

> You are welcome to quiz it,
> The penalty is
> That you add your own portrait
> For others to quiz.

And in a similar vein:

> I wish my album to contain
> The old familiar faces
> Of all my true and valued friends,
> They'll here find welcome places.

> And hope you'll not intrusive deem
> The request that now I make,
> A portrait true of each dear friend
> I ask for friendship's sake.

As usual, the satirical magazine *Punch* could not resist poking fun at the growing enthusiasm for trading cartes. It produced its own introductory carte with a rather different inscription, parodying the conventional verses:

> Yes, this is my album,
> And my affidavit,
> If you beg for one picture
> I'm blessed if you'll have it.

> And don't offer your own,
> But just take it for granted
> That if not in the book
> It's because you're not wanted.

Less commonly, the last carte in the album might also be decorated and inscribed with a verse encouraging the viewer to leave a carte for the next volume. Many of these introductory and end cartes are not credited to either a photographer or a publisher but those identified come predominantly from Ashford Brothers & Company, 76 Newgate Street, London; W. B. Prince, 3 Skinner Street, Snow Hill, London; and Burgowitz & Company, 43 Frith Street, Soho Square, London.

O. Henry Mace suggests that an established etiquette emerged with the arrangement of cartes within American albums. Many begin with a portrait of the president and other leading political figures (and, in the Civil War years, military leaders), followed by autographed images of friends and colleagues, with close family appearing towards the back of the album. Also towards the back would appear images of places visited, respected European figures (Queen

Left: *Cartes designed for the end of an album were rather more unusual. Although hand-coloured, this carte from an unidentified photographer may well be a pirated copy. The pictures surrounding the central verse were all issued as individual cartes, several of which bear the mark of E. Turner of Bungay, although it is unlikely that Turner produced them.*

Below: *Rarely is a collector fortunate enough to gain any biographical detail about the subject of a photograph. However, in this instance a fine portrait by Laurence of Cheltenham identifies the children as 'Rose Kennedy aged 7 years and 8 months and John Lane aged 6 years and 3 months'. The portrait was taken c.1863.*

Victoria was a particular favourite) and admired works of art. In Victorian Britain, no drawing room was considered complete without an album and British albums also tended to follow a similar etiquette. They commonly opened with pictures of the royal family and leading political figures. These would be followed in turn by individuals from the arts and literature and, in many cases, local clergy. Friends and family would follow at the rear of the album. In this way, the carte-de-visite album served a number of valuable functions: it recorded the genealogy of the family (and established its respectability) and also provided a rich source of entertainment and stimuli for conversation. Studied carefully by guests, the album indicated the tastes and prejudices of the host family, allowing the viewer to avoid embarrassing social gaffes.

In many ways, the drawing-room album offers a very personal and intimate insight into the values of a Victorian family. Today, many of the choices of image appear obscure and, indeed, many of the individual images are now unidentified, but much can still be learned. A study of the photographers represented among family portraits can offer clues to where the family lived and the extent of their personal contacts as well as their political and religious affiliations. Sadly, many albums are broken up by dealers who can make more money through the sale of individual images than whole albums.

In addition to the drawing-room album, many families also maintained a far more personal and less formalised album, often organised by one of the children of the family. These albums would usually contain only images of family and close friends and would be annotated with the name of the person responsible for maintaining the collection. For example, an album of thirty cartes bears this inscription on the inside cover:

Louisa Lea
with her younger Brothers
Jan. 4 1863
2 Cor: iii. 18

Frustratingly, the album contains no portraits of either Louisa or her brothers! Although the cartes within these family albums were generally very carefully, and properly, annotated with the subject's full name and title, there was also scope for humour, given the restricted audience for whom the album was intended. An album of fifty cartes from the Darbishire-Paget family includes

Servants and estate workers were often photographed at the wish of their employers. The firm of Bowen & Carpenter of Kilburn took this fine shot of 'Mr Coverdale's carriage and driver'. A number of other cartes from the same album show the butler and the gardener, both with their families. Despite the best efforts of the groom holding the horses, one has moved its head and the other appears to have twitched its ears, causing blurring in an otherwise very crisp image.

familiar family names (for example, Mrs Brace – 'Mia') and humorous comments (for example, a beautiful, vignetted portrait of a young girl is captioned simply 'The Little Woman'). Some captions can appear rather more pointed. The last carte in this particular album shows a rather rotund and stern-looking lady identified only as 'M.P. – The Wrecker'. Unfortunately, the meaning behind this apparently vitriolic reference is now lost. Both these albums give the impression of having been put together over a relatively short time. Others have evidently been compiled over a much longer period and, within such albums, it is possible to follow the growth and development of different family members, including marriages and other achievements.

Individual cartes could also be displayed in the home, and a wide variety of frames, viewers and other accessories was available. From the early 1860s, the market was flooded with all types of frame. The cheaper frames were made from thin sheet brass in two pieces joined by a sprung central bar which pulled the two halves together, clamping the image and a covering sheet of glass in

These more ornate frames help to illustrate the diversity of styles available. The double frame has brass 'elliptical' mats, which would suggest a date in the early 1860s. The frame at the top has two hinged wings which can be closed across the front of the image if required.

place. A further strip of brass was riveted approximately halfway up the central bar and could be pulled out to make a stand. While most of these mass-produced stands have no manufacturer's marks, one example studied bears the details 'H.G. Improved' stamped into the back. A variation on these cheaper frames involved the metal components being fixed with small nails to a wooden board the same size as the cartes-de-visite themselves. Although cheap, the impression of refinement was created by bevelling and gilding the edges of the glass cover plate. The majority of the frames of this type contain images of the mid to late 1860s.

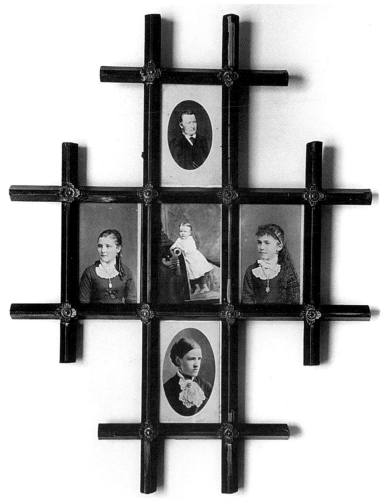

An ornate frame decorated with brass studs and designed to accommodate five cartes-de-visite. The portraits in the frame represent members of an American family from New York but are not original to the frame. The frame probably dates to the mid 1860s.

More expensive frames containing one, two or more cartes could be mounted on a wall. Wooden frames tended to replicate the characteristics of picture frames of the period and often it is only their size that identifies them as having been made for cartes. In the late 1860s, more rustic frames began to appear. Frames designed to accommodate multiple images (five is the largest number seen) were often embellished with gilt rosette studs. Other material used included carved bone and ivory.

When travelling away from home it was comforting to have close at hand cartes depicting loved ones, and, to facilitate this, travelling cases were produced.

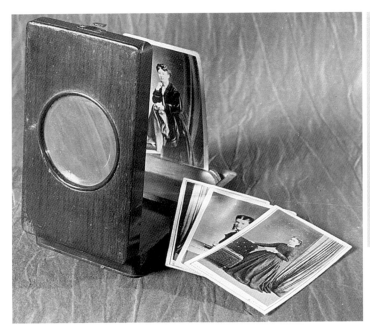

This viewer allowed people with failing eyesight to see their favourite cartes magnified through the lens at the front. Focus was obtained by moving the image forwards or backwards on an internal slide bar.

An example in the authors' collection was made of thin cardboard covered in fine leather and could accommodate two cartes side by side. The images were inserted into specially created sleeves and the whole case could be opened and stood up for display or closed up like a wallet and secured by a band of elasticated material which simply wrapped around it. The case bears the name 'Edwards & Jones, 161 Regent St'. Small albums were also available to hold only a limited number of images (normally eight). These albums could also be secured by a band of material wrapped around them.

To assist those with failing eyesight to view the cartes, a special viewer was available. The viewer was in the shape of a small box (approximately 3.5 by 6 inches or 90 by 150 mm) with a circular convex lens (2.5 inches or 60 mm in diameter) inserted into the top. The hinged top could be lifted up to reveal a sliding unit within the base into which a carte de visite could be inserted. By sliding the carte forwards or backwards, the image could be brought into sharp focus and magnified to aid viewing. When closed, there was sufficient room within the body of the viewer to store a small number of cartes.

Perhaps the most unusual use for a carte-de-visite was in a paperweight. A carte-sized piece of polished clear glass almost 1 inch (25 mm) thick, with carefully bevelled edges, had a piece of card secured to the base with a fine tape along three sides. The fourth side was left open to create a sleeve into which a carte could be inserted. The example in the authors' collection contained an image of Pope Pius IX when purchased.

An enormous range of comic cartes was produced to satisfy the ever increasing demand. Of
almost twenty in the authors' collection, many
bear the pasted labels of Frederick Passmore of
Cheapside, London ('Price 6d or Free by Post
for 7 Stamps'). At least three different label variations are in evidence. Topics for comic cartes
include the trials of parentage, the class structure, courtship and the actions of children. This
carte was produced c.1870.

THE PLEASURES OF MATRIMONY
OR
TWELVE MONTHS AFTER MARRIAGE.
Copyright.

Collecting, dating and preserving cartes-de-visite

Between three and four hundred million cartes were estimated to have been
sold annually at the height of their popularity. With photographer's studios set
up on every continent, it is small wonder that so many of these intriguing
images survive today, and in such good condition.

Given the number and diversity of cartes-de-visite available, it is possible to
assemble collections based on many different themes. Some collectors restrict
themselves to portraits of famous celebrities while others concentrate on the
work of particular photographers (for example, Mathew Brady or John Mayall).
Collections based on images from a certain area or town can provide a fascinating
and rewarding view of that location in the second half of the nineteenth century.
Some people collect the backplates rather than the images themselves while
others restrict their collections to particular periods (for example the period of
the crinoline). Those interested in the fashion of the time may collect only
images showing particular aspects of fashion in order to assemble a reference
collection that is more extensive and accessible than collections of original
garments. Pets in images (either alone or accompanied by their owners) can
provide a focus for a collection and at least one collector restricts himself to

The crinoline was a constant source of amusement for men. The magazine 'Punch' endlessly satirised the style, as did contemporary photographers. This carte is taken from a stereoscopic pair of images from the early 1860s and served two purposes: it poked gentle fun at the crinoline but also exposed a view of legs and underwear that bordered on the mildly erotic.

images of people reading. Topographic, nautical, military and architectural themes provide other fascinating areas for study.

Many antique shops and junk shops will have a few cartes available. Specialist antique fairs are good places to meet dealers and establish contacts. The details of these events can usually be found in the local press, or the local tourist information office should be able to help. Auctions often contain cartes among other items such as postcards. There are also a few specialist dealers who operate from premises that are open to the public. A gold mine of information and a vast array of images can be found at Jubilee Photographica, 10 Pierrepoint Row, Camden Passage, London, which is open on Wednesdays and Saturdays. A visit to the surrounding Camden Passage antiques market will often turn up other images as well.

What is certain is that there are a huge number of cartes available, many of which may be purchased at very low prices. As O. Henry Mace observes, 'Just as the carte was the "poor man's portrait" in the nineteenth century, it is now the poor man's collectible'. In 1999 it was still possible to find cartes-de-visite priced at less than £1.00, although rarer examples (for example portraits of royalty, politicians and other famous people) might cost up to £10.00 and particularly rare or unusual subjects (such as post-mortem images) may command rather higher prices.

The cheapest images tend to be unidentified portraits of ordinary people, which make up by far the greatest percentage of all cartes available. All too often these images are overlooked by collectors and a careful scrutiny can turn up a few surprises. In 1997 a very fine unmarked and probably pirated portrait of Confederate President Jefferson Davis was located in a pile of apparently ordinary images and purchased for just 25p. Although in most cases the subjects are unidentified, the images still provide an insight into the fashions and social conventions of the day and deserve more attention than they receive. On occasion, a carte may be annotated with the name of the sitter and a date, or it may give other information allowing a more intimate contact with the individual portrayed. One framed image of a robust young boy in the authors' collection bears the inscription 'Taken 1864 aged 5 years'; beneath is a further annotation, written in a different hand, stating 'Died Feb 26 1865 aged 5 years 10 months'. A fascinating group of cartes from the Hayward family (of Hayward's End, Stonehouse, Gloucestershire) is annotated with the name of each individual, their dates of birth and death, and also, where appropriate, the dates of their marriages and the names of their spouses. It is interesting to note that they almost all lived to a ripe old age and many survived well into their eighties. Another, otherwise uninspiring carte depicting a seated gentleman is brought to life when one reads on the back 'Rev. William Tapley Waymouth. Born 1811. Married 1837. Died at Basselbere, St. Kitts, W. Indies'. Unfortunately this amount of detail is very much the exception rather than the rule.

More expensive images include portraits of royalty, politicians and other famous characters of the day, military images (especially valuable if they depict weaponry), portraits of musicians and bands, sporting subjects and cartes depicting ordinary folk in their working clothes. In the case of images depicting royalty and other celebrities, care should be taken to see whether or not the portrait is credited to a particular photographer. Images without backmarks are generally pirated and therefore of lower value. Cartes depicting rural scenes, popular tourist attractions, beaches and historic sites and monuments are somewhat less expensive, as are images depicting art and statuary. The most expensive images tend to be the rarest – for example, the famous portrait of engineer Isambard Kingdom Brunel, in front of the huge anchor chains of the steamship *Great Eastern*, taken by Robert Howlett and published by the London Stereoscopic Company.

In the United States, cartes depicting unidentified private soldiers from the Civil War years could be purchased in 1999 for as little as $15. Cartes with weapons visible and those depicting identified officers – especially Confederates – are rather more collectible, especially if they bear the imprint of a particularly well-known photographer, for example Mathew Brady or Alexander Gardner. During the period August 1864 to August 1866, American cartes-de-visite were taxed by the Federal government and a variety of different tax stamps of different values were affixed to the cartes to prove that the tax had been paid. All images bearing such tax stamps are a little more valuable than those without because they can be dated to that particular period.

   With the exception of cartes with a Federal tax stamp, most images are difficult to date precisely even if they bear a date: there is no guarantee that the date given is the date on which the portrait was taken. Dates were sometimes added when a carte was presented to another person, as one inscription clearly demonstrates: 'We were pleased to receive your Carte. This is mine in return. Janet McGower. November 30th 1865'. A date might also commemorate the death of the individual or another event of importance.

   The card mounts can offer some guide in dating an image but, since many photographers routinely reprinted earlier negatives and copied much older daguerreotypes and ambrotypes, they can also be misleading. The earliest cartes were mounted on thin card (often cut to size by the photographer) with the photographer's name and address printed in several lines on the back. As time went on and the demand for cartes increased, the mounts increased in thickness and ornamentation and were produced pre-cut – in short, the more elaborate a mount, the later it is likely to be. In the United States, these early mounts were commonly decorated with a border of single or double gilt lines. Occasionally other colours were used instead. The use of borders remained uncommon in Europe.

   The thin card used on early mounts made them easy to slip into the sleeves in the albums but they were easily damaged and therefore, by 1870, different types of card mount were being introduced. Paste board, as the name suggests, was made by pasting together several layers of paper, with a better-quality

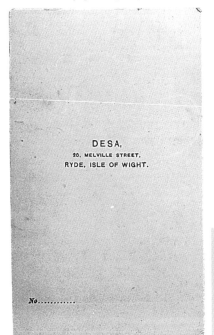

The earliest backmarks tended to be very simple with generally three lines of print giving the name of the photographer and the address. In this example from the studio of Desa, dating from the early 1860s, there is also a space at the bottom for the photographer to note the negative number in case of requests for further copies.

paper on the top and bottom. William Darrah notes that the most common paste boards used either five or seven layers of paper in their manufacture. Frequently at least one face of the mount was given a glazed finish known as 'enamelling'. Press board involved heavy machinery being used to press a single layer of material (often wood pulp with a binding agent) to a desired thickness and strength. Press board became widely available after 1875 although the quality (and consequent cost) varied considerably.

In Europe, the largest supplier of pre-cut and printed mounts was the company of A. Marion of Paris and London. By 1872, most American mounts were supplied by A. M. Collins & Son of Philadelphia, whose catalogues boasted three hundred types of pre-cut mount. Such monopolies understandably tended to standardise the styles and variations of carte mounts. Occasional novelty mounts were introduced although these tended to have a rather limited popularity. An example of such a novelty mount was introduced between 1866 and the 1870s with a variety of ornately decorated oval frames (some of which were made to look like hanging picture frames) into which a vignetted portrait could be pasted. One unusual variation on the theme (registered by 'Pumphrey: Birmingham') has a frame of coloured holly leaves surrounding a small oval portrait. The carte has the sentiment 'With the best wishes of the Season' printed around the holly frame (see page 16).

On the reverse side of the mount was the photographer's imprint. Some of the earliest imprints were simply pasted on to the mounts (a practice maintained

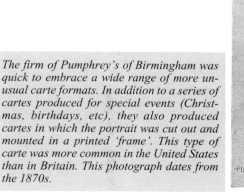

The firm of Pumphrey's of Birmingham was quick to embrace a wide range of more unusual carte formats. In addition to a series of cartes produced for special events (Christmas, birthdays, etc), they also produced cartes in which the portrait was cut out and mounted in a printed 'frame'. This type of carte was more common in the United States than in Britain. This photograph dates from the 1870s.

·PUMPHREY BROS PHOTOS 21, PARADISE ST. BIRM·

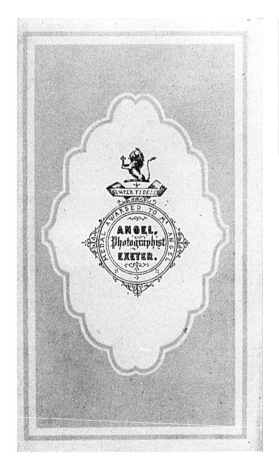

*By the mid 1860s, the pho-
tographer's name was often
placed within a decorative
vignette – in this case noting the
award of a photographic medal
to the photographer. In this example, the more elaborate photographer's mark is itself framed
within a larger space. This card
dates from the late 1860s.*

by a few photographers into the 1880s) but by mid to late 1860 details were normally printed on several lines, sometimes contained within a vignette. By 1867, the vignettes were becoming more and more ornate. Between 1864 and 1870, the reverse of some mounts was decorated with ornate patterning with a central ovoid left blank, into which the photographer's details were placed. Many photographers exhibited their work in national and international competitions and those receiving awards were naturally keen to advertise the fact. Where more than one award had been received, the details of all – including those won in previous years – were shown on the back of their cartes. The date of the latest award can therefore be used as a guide to the date of the image.

Although the carte mounts can offer an indication of the date of an image (subject to the limitations already outlined), a working knowledge of fashions of the period can provide the collector with a potentially more reliable guide. A brief outline of period fashion is included as an introduction to the subject.

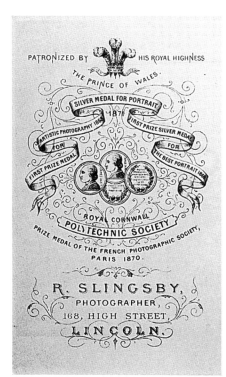

As a general rule of thumb, the more elaborate the backmark, the later the date. In this example from the studio of R. Slingsby, the photographer has gone to great lengths to draw attention to the range of medals he has been awarded and his royal patronage. Given the dates of the medals, it is apparent that this card dates from the mid 1870s.

Rarely does a card bear a date that can be ascribed with confidence to the taking of the portrait, but in this example the space for the negative number has been extended to include the date on which the negative was registered – August 1863.

Women's costume in cartes of the late 1850s to early 1860s is characterised by dome-shaped skirts. These skirts were supported by a cage-crinoline, and extra width was often added with numerous flounces. The hair was worn with a centre parting. It was drawn over the ears, where it sometimes puffed out, and was made into a coil or chignon at the back. Hairnets were a common accessory.

The shape of the skirt became more pyramidal, until, by the mid 1860s, skirts were flatter in front, with the bulk of the skirt shifting towards the back. The numerous flounces were discarded, and skirts were often plain or simply trimmed along the hem. However, bolder arabesque or geometric decoration was also fashionable. By the late 1860s, the shaped skirt developed a train at the back, and a half-crinoline or stiffened petticoats were worn underneath. The hairstyle now left the ears exposed and was drawn into a larger chignon.

A good knowledge of fashion trends can help to date images. The fullness on this skirt sweeps towards the back; this is typical of the early to mid 1860s. The shaped sleeve, called a two-piece coat sleeve, first appeared just after 1860. It is topped with an epaulette and is worn with a white undersleeve. Patterned ribbon trims the outfit.

A double skirt became common from 1865. From about 1868, the overskirt was bunched high at the back over a bustle, with an apron-effect at the front. The two skirts were often elaborately flounced. The coiffure increased in height and elaboration, and the chignon became even larger.

The bustle began to lose its popularity from 1873, and long fitted bodices were introduced. The silhouette became increasingly slender and, by 1875, it developed into a style of dress called the 'tie-back'. The fullness at the back dropped to below hip level and lengthened into a train. A small standing collar was fashionable in the 1880s, increasing in height for the rest of the century. By the mid 1880s, the bustle was revived, but this time it was a high, horizontal bustle. The coiffure became plainer once more, with the addition of a short, curled fringe *c.*1880.

The double skirt is typical of the style which appeared c.1868. At this time, the underskirt was bunched high at the back over a bustle, and both skirts were heavily flounced.

.J F TRULL   FALMOUTH

Men's clothes became looser in cut during the late 1850s and early 1860s. The morning coat, a high-buttoning coat cut away in a curve over the hips, was replacing the frock-coat in popularity, as were informal coats such as the lounge jacket. Coats could be either single- or double-breasted. They were worn with trousers and a waistcoat, which also buttoned high. The coat, waistcoat and trousers were often all of different cloth, although matching suits, called 'dittos', were also worn.

For sports, men wore the morning coat or lounge jacket, teamed with knickerbockers. In 1866, the Norfolk shirt made its appearance for sportswear. This was a loose jacket with big vertical pleats caught in at the waist, and it, too, was worn with knickerbockers. The Norfolk suit increased in popularity throughout the rest of the century.

During the 1870s, lounge coats were close-fitting. The double-breasted form of the lounge coat, called a 'reefer jacket', was particularly popular. A greater variety of hats appeared. In addition to the popular top hat, informal hats such as the deerstalker and a precursor of the bowler hat made their appearance.

The style of the children's clothes imitates that of adults. The cut of the boy's suit is the same as men's suits from the 1860s. More obvious is the short crinoline worn by the girl. This implies a date c.1860–6.

This image highlights the need to be cautious when relying on costume in order to date images. In group photographs, more old-fashioned styles are often seen on elderly women. In this image, the woman on the left wears the double skirt fashionable c.1865–8 (just prior to the introduction of the bustle) while the woman on the right is more plainly dressed and coiffured in fashions of the early to mid 1860s. Despite this, the dress and hairstyle of the woman on the left indicate that the earliest possible date for this carte is 1865.

This girl's frock imitates the apron-fronted costume worn by adult women in the 1870s. Curled fringes appeared during the mid to late 1870s, making that the most probable date for this carte.

Shirt collars in the 1860s and 1870s were low. They were single or double and were worn with a cravat. The cravat was a narrow band of material in the 1860s, either tied in a bow or fastened with a pin. The collars grew higher in the 1880s, and the tie became a narrow, shaped band of material, knotted or tied in a bow.

Boys and girls up to the age of five or six were dressed in short frocks with round necklines and short sleeves. White frocks were usually embroidered in openwork called *broderie anglaise*. Frocks trimmed with braid in arabesque patterns were fashionable in the 1860s. The frocks were worn with sashes, tied either around the waist or over the shoulder. In the 1870s and 1880s the cut of these frocks echoed that of women's clothes. Throughout the period, frocks were also made out of many different fabrics. Plaids were popular up to the 1870s.

During the 1860s, straight or gathered knickerbockers were worn by boys between the ages of three and ten. They were teamed with a waistcoat and open jacket, or with a loose, belted tunic. Sometime between the ages of seven and ten, long trousers replaced knickerbockers. Longer single- or double-breasted jackets were popular in the 1870s, and the Norfolk jacket replaced the tunics worn earlier. Short jackets, worn with waistcoats, appeared in the 1880s. Velvet party suits, worn with lace collars, were popularised by Frances Hodgson Burnett's story *Little Lord Fauntleroy* (1886). The book's hero wore one in black velvet, and this style of party suit became known as the 'Fauntleroy' suit. In the late 1860s and 1870s the Scotch or Highland suit was popular for young boys. Sailor suits were first worn in the late 1850s and increased in popularity right through to the end of the century.

Girls' dresses imitated women's clothing until the early 1880s. Overskirts and bustle effects were worn in the 1870s and early 1880s. Loose dresses, similar to the tunics worn by boys, appeared in the 1880s. They were belted, or gathered into a waistband, and were called blouses. The fullness at the shoulders was taken in, either into a yoke or by smocking. Pinafores were common at this time and girls, like boys, also wore sailor suits.

There remains, however, a need to be cautious when using costume to date cartes-de-visite. Fashionable cuts took longer to reach certain areas. Poorer people may have worn their clothes for as long as they remained serviceable, and even their 'best' may have been old-fashioned. Some people, particularly older men and women, adhered to previous styles. An analysis of fashion is a guide to the *earliest possible* date of a carte-de-visite. For example, a carte showing a woman in an apron-fronted bustle dress could not date from before *c*.1868.

Having begun to collect cartes-de-visite, it is important to consider their storage. It is easy to become complacent about their durability when one sees images almost as perfect as the day they left the photographer's studio. However, cartes can be easily damaged and it must be remembered that, no matter what their monetary value, each one is a piece of photographic and social history

20, NORTH STREET,
GUILDFORD & CHERTSEY R.ᵈ
W O K I N G.

The tall, elaborately trimmed hat was fashionable in the mid to late 1880s. The short, fitted jacket and long fur boa also date from this period. Folds on the skirt indicate that the woman wears a bustle, revived from the mid 1880s.

deserving of our respect. Many may be unique.

As a simple rule of thumb, the less an image is handled, the less damage it is likely to sustain. If images are bought as part of a complete album, then, where possible, it is important to maintain the integrity of the collection. Frequent removal of cartes from albums, and their subsequent insertion, can cause damage to both the image and the fragile album sleeves. Each carte in turn should be removed and carefully documented before being replaced. Details to record should include:

- the subject (for example, seated female facing left)
- the condition of the image and mount (noting any obvious damage)
- the dimensions and thickness of the card mount
- embellishments to the mount (such as whether the corners are rounded or square, the texture, and so on)
- the photographer's name and address and any other details provided
- a description of the photographer's logo (if there is one)
- any annotations on the carte

The addition of any further notes directly on to the carte, or to album pages, is not recommended. However, if the album is falling apart, it may be appropriate to number the individual pages. This and any other identification should be added lightly, using a soft pencil, near the edge of the page. Separate album pages (whether individually or still within an intact album) can be afforded a measure of protection by the insertion of a sheet of acid-free paper between each page. The best way to store individual images is in clear melinex (mylar) sleeves. These can be obtained from specialist shops which sell storage albums with pages divided into four compartments, ideal for storing cartes-de-visite.

The use of such sleeves allows both sides of the image to be studied without direct handling. Oils from the skin and the abrasive action of dust particles can cause irreparable damage to an image. Given the poor quality of many early card mounts, damage is easy and permanent. These early mounts tended to be highly acidic (a result of their manufacture) and this can have an adverse effect on any images stored in direct contact with them, making good storage essential. It is equally important to ensure that cartes are stored in a dry environment: tintypes especially will rust in conditions of high humidity. Rust will cause the image to lift off the plate and will also damage the mount. Other images can also be adversely affected by mould and mildew brought about by damp conditions. Tintypes can also be damaged by pressure which can cause the plate to bend. If this happens, the protective varnish may flake off, taking the image with it. Many specialist collectors' shops stock melinex sleeves and albums and these can also be purchased by mail order from the Taunton Stamp Shop, 66 Bridge Street, Taunton, Somerset TA1 1UD (telephone: 01823 283327).

Where possible, cartes-de-visite should be stored in the dark to avoid damage caused by prolonged exposure to ultra-violet light from direct sunlight and fluorescent light. Lengthy exposure will cause the image to fade. Conservation of photographs is a highly skilled and complex task which should never be attempted by the amateur collector. There is much to be said for the old adage 'Prevention is better than cure'!

Further reading

On the history of portrait and general photography
Coe, Brian. *The Birth of Photography: The Story of the Formative Years 1800–1900*. Spring Books, London, 1989.
Darrah, William C. *The Carte-de-Visite in Nineteenth Century Photography*. Self-published, Gettysburg, 1981.
Dimond, F., and Taylor, R. *Crown and Camera: The Royal Family and Photography 1842–1910*. Penguin, Harmondsworth, 1987.
Gernsheim, Helmut. *The Rise of Photography: 1850–1880*. Thames & Hudson,1988.
Hannavy, John. *Victorian Photographers at Work*. Shire, 1997.
Horan, James D. *Mathew Brady: Historian with a Camera*. Crown Publishers, New York, 1955.
Linkman, Audrey. *The Victorians: Photographic Portraits*. Tauris Parke Books, London, 1993.
MacDonald, Gus. *Camera: A Victorian Eyewitness*. Batsford, 1979.
Thomas, Alan. *The Expanding Eye: Photography and the Nineteenth Century Mind*. Croom Helm, London, 1978.

On nineteenth-century fashions
Bradfield, Nancy. *Costume in Detail 1730–1930*. Harrap,1983.
Buck, Anne. *Victorian Costume*. Ruth Bean, Bedford, 1984.
Cunnington, Phillis, and Buck, Anne. *Children's Costume in England 1300–1900*. A. & C. Black, 1972.
Gernsheim, Alison. *Victorian and Edwardian Fashion: A Photographic Survey*. Dover, New York, 1981.
Ginsburg, Madeleine. *Victorian Dress in Photographs*. Batsford, 1988.
Lansdell, Avril. *Fashion à la Carte 1860–1900*. Shire,1985; reprinted 1992.

On collecting and conserving cartes-de-visite
Mace, O. Henry. *Collector's Guide to Early Photographs*. Wallace-Homestead, Radnor, Pennsylvania, 1990.
Martin, Elizabeth. *Collecting and Preserving Old Photographs*. Collins, 1988.
McCulloch, Lou W. *Card Photographs: A Guide to Their History and Value*. Schiffer, Exton, Pennsylvania, 1981.

Places to visit

Many museums now include some cartes-de-visite among their displays, but major collections can be seen at:

The National Museum of Photography, Film and Television, Pictureville, Bradford, West Yorkshire BD1 1NQ. Telephone: 01274 727488. (Their material includes the former Science Museum collection and the Kodak Museum collection among others.)

The Royal Photographic Society, Milsom Street, Bath, Somerset BA1 1DN. Telephone: 01225 462841. Website: www.rps.org (A permanent exhibition on the early years of photography with temporary displays of contemporary and historic material.)

The Victoria and Albert Museum, Cromwell Road, South Kensington, London SW7 2RL. Telephone: 020 7942 2000. Website: www.vam.ac.uk (Houses a substantial collection of cartes.)

The Scottish National Portrait Gallery, 1 Queen Street, Edinburgh EH2 1JD. Telephone: 0131 624 6200. Website: www.natgalscot.ac.uk (Home to the Scottish Photography Archive.)

Further information

The Photographic Collectors Club of Great Britain (PCCGB), 5 Station Industrial Estate, Low Prudhoe, Northumberland NE42 6NP, is an excellent way of making contact with other collectors. The Club holds meetings around Britain, organises regional collectors' fairs throughout the year and one national fair (named 'Photographica') in London each spring. Members receive a quarterly newsletter and journal.

Index

Note: italicised numbers refer either to illustrations or to information contained within captions.

Advertising cartes *18*, 18
Aguado, Count 13
Alabama (ship) *62*
Albert, Prince 35, *35*, 36, 56
Albumen 10, 12
Album portraits 74
Albums for CDVs 74 -6
Alexandra, Princess of Wales *34*, 35
Allen, A.M. 40
Ambrotypes *10*, 10-12, 20, 74
American Civil War 12, 14, *15*, 40, 58, 63, 78, 87
American process 12
Angel, photographer *90*
Anthony, E. & A.T. *41*, 58, *59*
Appleton & Co *47*
Arthur, Prince *46*
Artists and photography 69
Art studies 5
Ashford Brothers & Co 43, *57*, 78
Atlantic Monthly 33
Backdrops *26*, 26, *27*, 28
Backplates 21, 37, *88*, 88, 89, *90*, 90, *91*
Baker, Edmund *56*
Balls, F. *56*
Barnardo, Dr Thomas John 64, 66
Barnum, P.T. 9
Bassano, Alexander 14
Beard, Richard 8
Beau, Adolphe *18*
Bedford, F. 68
Bernhardt, Sarah *38*, 38, 39
Biographical detail on CDVs 87
Bismarck, Otto von *37*, 57, 63
Blanquart, Evrard Louis-Désiré 12
Booth, John Wilkes 37, *58*
Bowen & Carpenter 80
Brady, Mathew 9, 37, *41*, 41, *58*, 58, 59, 85, 87
Brass mats and preservers 7, 7, *10*, *11*, *13*, *20*

Brides 29, 50, *51*
British Empire 57, 66, 67
Brockmann, F. & O. 72, 73
Brogi, Giocomo 72
Brookes of Manchester 30
Brooks, W. 68
Brown, Ford Madox 69
Brunel, Isambard Kingdom 9, 87
Burgwitz & Co *77*, 78
Burnett, Frances Hodgson 96
Burn-out 52
Cabinet portraits 16, 76
Cade, R. *28*
Calotypes 9
Camden Passage antiques 86
Camera obscura 6, 9
Cann, John *55*
Carbon print process 19
Card mounts 88
Carlyle, Thomas 38
Cartomania 5, 74
Celebrity CDVs 33-43
Chadwick, Edwin 55
Chancellor of Sackville Street 25
Children in CDVs *25*, *26*, 26, *44*, 44-50, *94*, 95, *96*
'Children of the Battlefield' 61-3
Children's toys as props *46*, 46
Chit, Francis 38
Christie, Agatha 5
Chromotype process *17*, 19
Churchill, G. 38
Claudet, Antoine 7, 8
Cobb, J.V. *71*
Collecting CDVs 85-7
Collins, A.M. & Son 89
Collodion 10
Collodion positive 10, 11
Colour distortion 29
Colouring CDVs 29, 32
Comic portraits *30*, *31*, 32, 73, *85*

Composite images *43*
Converting tintypes to CDV format 14
Cooley, Sam A. *61*
Cooper, Montague *17*
Copying services *19*, 20
Cost of CDVs 14, *16*, 19
Costume and dating 92-7
Cricket *32*, 32
Crimean War 58
Crinoline dresses 26, 85, *86*, *92*, 92
Cromwell, Oliver *42*
Crystal Palace *18*, 18
Cutting, James 10
Daguerre, Louis-Jacques Mandé 6-9
Daguerreotypes *6*, 6, 7, 9, 11, 12, *20*, 20, 29, 37, 74
Darrah, William 33, 37, 42, 49, 72, 89
Dating CDVs 88-97
Davis, Jefferson *59,* 87
Death and photography 49-50, 55-6
Défossé, photographer 65
Deibert, H.S. 20
Delaroche, Paul 21
Delensert, E. 13
Desa, photographer 88
Diamond cameo portrait *18*, 18, 19, 76
Dickens, Charles *39*
Disdéri & Co *12*, 13, *33*, 33, 34, 42
Disraeli, Benjamin *39*, 39, 40
Dodero, Louis 13
Dodson, photographer 16
Dorffel, Theodore 7
Downey, W. & D. *34*, 35, 38, 39
Duryea, J. *25*
Earnings from CDV sales 34
Edwards & Jones *1,* 84
Eisenmann, Charles 41
Elgin, Earl of *33*
Elisabeth, Empress of Austria 36, 37
End of album CDVs *79*
Ethics in photography 61, 64
Execution of the Emperor Maximilian 71
Famous portrait collections 9
Fenton, Roger 36, 58, 69
Ferrotypes 11
Festive CDVs 16, *17*
Fisherwomen 27, 54, *68*, 68
Flament, J. *42*

Florida (ship) *62*
Fowx, Egbert G. 14, 20
Fox Talbot, William Henry 9, 12
Frames for CDVs 81-3
Franco-Prussian War *34*, 37, 54, 63, 64
Fredericks, C.D. & Co *60*
French Product Exposition (1844) 7
Fry, W. & A.H. *54*
Gardner, Alexander 59, 60, 61, 64, 87
Garibaldi, Giuseppe *57*
Gem photographs 14, 15
Gernsheim, Helmut 13, 40
Gettysburg, Battle of 59, 60
Ghémar Frères *4*
Giroux, Alphonse 6
Gladstone, W.E. 40
Goddard, John 8
Godfrey, George W. & Co *15*
Goodfellow, E. *19*, *69*
Goston, João *62*
Gouraud, François 9
Gowell's Anastic Press 75
Great Eastern 87
Great Western 9
Haddy, W. *45*
Handel Triennial Festival *18*, 18
Harris, John *41*
Harrison's of Falmouth 16, *17*, 18
Harrow School *31*
Hawke, J. *23*
Haycraft, J. *67*
Hayler, Henry 66
Heath, Vernon *67*
Helena, Princess *36*
Henderson, A.L. 23
Hildyard, Walter *46*
Hills and Saunders *31*, 38, *51*
Historic monuments 67, 68
Holmes, Oliver Wendell 33, 58
Horner, M. *70*
Howlett, Robert 87
Hughes, Arthur 39
Hughes, Cornelius Jabez 22
Hughes, Marc 53
Illustrated London News 8
Industrial Revolution 72
Introductory CDVs for albums *76, 77,* 77, 78

Itinerant photographers 12, *27*, 48
Japan *67*, 67
Johnson, Andrew *59*
Jones, Frederick *34, 62*
Joyner, J. *52*
Jubilee Photographica 86
Kaulbach, W.V. *50*
Kaunitzer, Jacob *30*
Kimbolton Castle 75
Ladmore & Son *49*
La Lumière 13
Laurence, photographer *79*
Lee, General Robert E. *58, 60*
Lenthall, H. *39, 44*
Leopold, Prince *46*
Lerebours, N.P. 6
Licence fee for daguerreotypes 8
Lincoln, Abraham 12, 37, *58*
Linkman, Audrey 52
Littlefield Parsons & Co *8*
London Stereoscopic and Photographic Co 39, *59, 65, 73*, 87
Louise, Princess 4
Mace, O. Henry 78, 86
Madonna and Child 72
Manassas, Battle of 58, *63*
Manet, Edouard 71
Mann, F.S. *70*
Marion & Co, wholesalers 4, 34, 35, 38, 89
Martin, Adolphé 11
Mason, W.O. *64*
Masonic insignia *65*
Masury & Hartshorn 37
Mayall, John 8, *22*, 26, 29, 32, 34, *35*, 35, *36, 46*, 85
McAllister & Bros 63
Meinerth, Carl 29
Melinex (mylar) sleeves 98
Mendelssohn, Albert *37*
Merritt, Thomas *60*
Mezzo-tinto method 29
Micro-photographs *65*
Millais, John Everett 69, 71
Montages (see also *Composite images*) 42
Morris, Jane 69
Morris, William 69

Mountain, William *48*
Musical CDV albums 76
Musicians *28, 31, 48*
Napoleon Bonaparte 64
Napoleon III 33, *34*, 34, 63, 64
National Gazette 57
Neck clamps *23, 45*
Negretti & Zambra *18*, 18
Nelson of Bywater *30*
Niépce, Joseph Nicéphore 6, 10
Niépce de Saint Victor, Abel 10
Nude photography 8
O'Sullivan, Timothy 59, 60
Paperweights with CDVs 84
Paris, siege of 64, *65*
Parry, John *30*
Passmore, Frederick *85*
Paste board mounts 88
Peck, Samuel 11
Permanent carbon process *17*, 19
Pets in photographs 47
Petzal, Josef *7*
Photographic Art Publishing Institute 72
Photographic drawings 9
Photographic Journal 70
Photographic News 21, 34, 35, 36, 66
Photographic props *23*, 26, 27, *46*, 46
Photomontage 42, *43*
Pirated images *34*, 35, 38, 72, *76*, 87
Pius IX, Pope 84
Plastic cases 14
Plumbe, John 9
Poe, Edgar Allan 37
Pornography 66
Portier, C. *66*
Portrait poses 22-5, 51, *52*, 52
Post-mortem photography *49*, 49
Potter's Patent sleeves 14
Practical Mechanics' Journal 13
Pre-Raphaelite movement 69-71
Press board mounts 89
Prince, W.B. 78
Principles and Practice of Photography 22
'Proscribed Royalist' (painting) *71*
Protective card sleeves *14*
Provost & Co 68
Pumphrey of Birmingham *16, 89*, 89

Punch 21, 24, 24, 78, *86*
Purpose of portraiture 21, 22
Raphael *72*
Recording CDVs 98
Reeves, A. *53*
Regional costume 27, 54, *66, 68*, 68
Rejlander, Oscar 27
Restoring CDVs *19*
Retouching 29
Roberts, F.J. 43
Robinson, Henry Peach 38
Robinson, Peter 18
Rogers, H.J. 24
Root, Marcus *6*, 10, 29
Rosmer, A.W. *91*
Rossetti, Dante Gabriel 39, 69
Rowe, Thomas *55*
Royal Institute, London 9
Royal Society 9
Ruskin, John 39, 70
Saltwood Castle *71*
Samurai *67*
Sarony, Napoleon *38*
Schauer, Gustav *72*, 72
School photographs 32, 47, *48*
Scott, William Bell 39
Scott Archer, Frederick 10
Seldon, W.D. & Co *63*
Services offered by studios 20
Silsbee, Case & Co. 37
Silver nitrate 9
Slavery 63
Slingsby, R. *91*
Smith, William 64
Social awareness and photography 64, 66
Social function of CDV albums 79-80
Spencer & Downs *16*
Spirit photography 56
Sporting portraits *31, 32*, 32
Steigler, Rudolph *34*

Stereoscopic images *86*
Stiles, Henry *28*
Stockwell Orphanage Handbell Ringers *48*
Storing CDVs 98
Stratton, Charles *41*
Stratton, Lavinia Warren *41*
Sure cards 38
Swan, J.W. 19
Talbotypes 9
Taunton Stamp Shop 98
Tax stamps on CDVs *40*, 40, 87
Thomas, Alan 36
Thumb, General Tom *41*
Times, The 53, 53
Tintypes *11*, 11, 12, 14
Tissue paper covers *4, 17*
Tourism and photography 68
Tournier, H. *42*
Trade lists 37
Travelling CDV cases *1*, 83, 84
Turner, E. *79*
Union cases 7, *8*, 11
Victoria, Queen 34-6, 38, 40, 56, 79
Victoria and photography 36
Viewers for CDVs *84*, 84
Voightlander 7
Waterloo, Battle of 64
Wedding dresses 50, *51*
Wet-plate process 10
Wholesalers 34, 36, 37, 38
Wilcox, H. 14, 19, 46
Wildman & Sons *70*
William, Kaiser of Germany 64
Window, F.R. 18, 76
Wing's Patent Multiplying Camera *15*, 16
Wood-frame cases 7, 11, 14
Works of art in photography 71-3
Wynter, Dr Andrew 29